HAZARDOUS
TO OUR
HEALTH?

HAZARDOUS TO OUR HEALTH?

FDA REGULATION OF HEALTH CARE PRODUCTS

Edited by
Robert Higgs

Foreword by Joel J. Nobel

The INDEPENDENT INSTITUTE

Oakland, California

THE INDEPENDENT INSTITUTE
100 Swan Way
Oakland CA 94621
510-632-1366 fax 510-568-6040
ISBN : 0-945999-41-0 http://www.independent.org

Hazardous to Our Health? : FDA regulation of health care products / edited by Robert Higgs ; foreword by Joel J. Nobel

Includes references and index.

Manufactured in the United States of America.
Library of Congress Catalog Card Number 95-80320
International Standard Book Number (paper) 0-945999-41-0

INDEPENDENT STUDIES IN POLITICAL ECONOMY:

THE ACADEMY IN CRISIS
The Political Economy of Higher Education
Edited by John W. Sommer
Foreword by Nathan Glazer

AGRICULTURE AND THE STATE
Market Processes and Bureaucracy
E. C. Pasour, Jr.
Foreword by Bruce L. Gardner

ALIENATION AND THE SOVIET ECONOMY
The Collapse of the Socialist Era
Paul Craig Roberts
Foreword by Aaron Wildavsky

ANTITRUST AND MONOPOLY
Anatomy of a Policy Failure
D. T. Armentano
Foreword by Yale Brozen

ARMS, POLITICS AND THE ECONOMY
Historical and Contemporary Perspectives
Edited by Robert Higgs
Foreword by William A. Niskanen

BEYOND POLITICS
Markets, Welfare, and the Failure of Bureaucracy
William C. Mitchell and Randy T. Simmons
Foreword by Gordon Tullock

THE DIVERSITY MYTH
"Multiculturalism" and the Politics of Intolerance at Stanford
David O. Sacks and Peter A. Thiel
Foreword by Elizabeth Fox-Genovese

FREEDOM, FEMINISM AND THE STATE
Edited by Wendy McElroy
Foreword by Lewis Perry

OUT OF WORK
Unemployment and Government in Twentieth-Century America
Richard K. Vedder and Lowell E. Gallaway
Foreword by Martin Bronfenbrenner

PRIVATE RIGHTS & PUBLIC ILLUSIONS
Tibor R. Machan
Foreword by Nicholas Rescher

REGULATION AND THE REAGAN ERA
Politics, Bureaucracy and the Public Interest
Edited by Roger E. Meiners and Bruce Yandle, Jr.
Foreword by Robert W. Crandall

TAXING ENERGY
Oil Severance Taxation and the Economy
Robert Deacon, Stephen DeCanio, H. E. Frech, III, and M. Bruce Johnson
Foreword by Joseph P. Kalt

For further information and a catalog of publications, please contact:

THE INDEPENDENT INSTITUTE
100 Swan Way
Oakland, CA 94621
Phone: 510-632-1366   Fax: 510-568-6040
http://www.independent.org

The INDEPENDENT INSTITUTE

THE INDEPENDENT INSTITUTE is a non-profit, scholarly research and educational organization which sponsors comprehensive studies on the political economy of critical social and economic problems.

The politicization of decision-making in society has largely confined public debate to the narrow reconsideration of existing policies. Given the prevailing influence of partisan interests, little social innovation has occurred. In order to understand both the nature of and possible solutions to major public issues, the Independent Institute's program adheres to the highest standards of independent inquiry and is pursued regardless of prevailing political or social biases and conventions. The resulting studies are widely distributed as books and other publications, and are publicly debated through numerous conference and media programs.

Through this uncommon independence, depth, and clarity, the Independent Institute pushes at the frontiers of our knowledge, redefines the debate over public issues, and fosters new and effective directions for government reform.

Contents

Foreword

This powerful book focuses on the recurring questions of whether patients benefit more from a government-dominated, centralized decision-making system to regulate the safety and efficacy of medical products or from a decentralized system in which physicians and patients make the decisions for themselves. The FDA's position has long been that physicians and patients are free to choose only from among the alternatives the FDA has approved. While the FDA has seldom approved a product that is unsafe or ineffective, it has attracted critics because of its delays in approval, which may keep beneficial products off the market, and because of the more general effect of FDA regulations in raising research and development (R&D) costs, and therefore reducing innovation. As a more activist FDA has increasingly limited the scope of private decisions through stricter controls on products, advertising, and the dissemination of information over the past 5 to 10 years, the FDA's *product regulation* mandate has, increasingly, become in effect, *regulation of the practice of medicine.* This process has not yet been openly debated and decided upon at a national policy level, but has, instead, resulted from regulatory "creep."

The FDA's intention has been to foreclose decisions by individual physicians and patients that are likely to prove harmful, but the agency's regulations have sometimes foreclosed or delayed availability of beneficial options. Whether one judges the overall outcome of the FDA's actions satisfactory depends in part on whether one places a higher value on individual freedom *per se* (i.e. on a principle) or on the actual medical results and benefits. The freedom to be wrong will also harm patients.

I believe it is possible to operate a centralized regulatory system that helps to ensure the safety and efficacy of marketed products, but to do so, the FDA must overcome serious challenges of method, organizational discipline, quality of judgment, and learning from experience. Unfortunately, in the United States, medical product regulation is very politicized, and regulatory science is undermined too much and too often by our uniquely adversarial culture of squabbling and grandstanding politicians, advocacy groups, attorneys, media sensationalists, and self-interested health professionals.

In general, I prefer competition in most activities because it provides better results for consumers. Some recently proposed schemes for privatizing FDA product reviews, however, may or may not create more problems than they solve. One wonders, for instance, whether effective competition can occur if the FDA itself accredits private testing laboratories—its own competitors. It will simply be extending its control over a sector that is not yet regulated.

There can be little question that the peculiar natural law of bureaucracies includes the drive to grow in size and power in response to proof of their deficiencies. Government bureaucracies have a perverse incentive. All failures are explained in terms of resource constraints. In the past, Congress has rewarded the FDA for its failure by allocating the agency more money and personnel.

Outside government failure and resource constraints stimulate examination of methods and lead to changes in *how* things are done. Although they may not yet be visible to the public, some constructive changes have been made at the FDA in recent years. But internal improvements focused on efficiency does not necessarily equal faster or better decision making; these derive from experience, from institutionalizing what has been learned from experience, and continuous reengineering. Here, the FDA is limited by its organizational structure and value system.

We are unlikely to see any long-term progress until the FDA embraces the possibility that it can and does make mistakes. Learning from experience requires recognizing and admitting error. The FDA culture discourages that realization and, therefore, the agency continues to err. It is irrelevant whether one perceives this refusal to admit error as bureaucratic arrogance or as a fearful institutional response to repeated beatings by Congress and the media. It is unacceptable organizational behavior because it presupposes that, when there is conflict over data, analysis, or action, only the FDA can be right! It is this characteristic that so greatly antagonizes competent outsiders, industry included. A doctrine of FDA infallibility is not acceptable regardless of how rarely the agency makes a mistake.

The people I know at the FDA—specifically in the Center for Devices and Radiological Health—are intelligent, sensitive, and committed. But admitting error in a politically charged environment is difficult when the institutional culture does not support it. Until the possibility of error is comfortably accepted, experience will fail to instruct, and poor judgments will occur.

At the heart of the regulatory dilemma is the merging of a scientific bureaucracy with police functions. Giving scientists police power is unwise. Allowing cops to create their own science to justify their actions is risky. Coupling science, police power, and a doctrine of infallibility is a fundamentally flawed national policy that is extremely dangerous. Even though specific cases of abuse of power are limited in number, they appear to have grown more frequent since the passage of the Safe Medical Devices Act in 1990. In the ultimate analysis, too much power exists in one place and among too few people. Effective external safeguards and genuine separation of powers would contribute significantly to reducing the dangers of excessive centralization of police powers in the hands of the FDA. At a minimum an independent external "police" review board and binding arbitration of disputes deserve serious consideration.

Hazardous to Our Health? examines the issues from a rarely voiced and considered viewpoint. The history of the FDA's growth to power is accurate, and the insights offered are provocative. Those insights will, inevitably, become a critical part of the national debate about FDA reform and contribute to its vital balance and the welfare of patients.

—Joel J. Nobel, M.D.
President, ECRI

Acknowledgments

This volume is a product of the Center for Health Policy Innovation at the Independent Institute. As with all of the Institute's publications, *Hazardous to Our Health?* owes its genesis to Institute president David Theroux and his unwavering support for public policy studies that meet high standards of scholarship. I am also greatly indebted to Theresa Navarro, director of program services at the Institute, for her superb management of the manuscript through its successive stages of production.

This book was made possible by the generous support of the Marti Nelson Cancer Research Foundation, and *Hazardous to Our Health?* is dedicated to the memory of the late Marti Nelson, M.D.

—Robert Higgs, Ph.D.
Research Director
The Independent Institute

1

Introduction

Robert Higgs

The U.S. Food and Drug Administration (FDA) is one of the most powerful federal regulatory agencies, if not *the* most powerful. It routinely makes decisions that seal the fates of millions of people in the United States and around the world. Although the general public, which knows little about the agency's actual operations, gives it a high approval rating, independent experts have a quite different opinion of it. Recently, Dr. Joel J. Nobel, perhaps the world's leading authority on medical technology, told a conference audience, "This country has a new public health problem—Congress and the FDA."[1] James O. Page, publisher and editor in chief of *JEMS (Journal of Emergency Medical Services)*, recently wrote, "We will surely live to regret the day we gave the FDA the kind of arbitrary power it is now exercising" (Page 1992, 91). Many other authorities, cited in the studies below, share these opinions. Indeed, some experts hold the FDA responsible for hundreds of thousands of deaths that, absent its regulations, might have been avoided.

We have here a paradox, a government agency created and maintained to protect the public health, yet one whose actual operations have the opposite effect, causing enormous harm to the public health—not to speak of its other pernicious effects, including a far-reaching suppression of liberty.

Before proceeding to detailed studies, let us consider briefly three important questions: (1) How has the FDA acquired its vast powers? Because it is an agency created by politicians and operated by bureaucrats, this question relates to the political process. (2) Why is the FDA bound to fail to achieve its ostensible goals? This question pertains to the limitations of any attempt at social central planning, of which the agency is an example. (3) How does the FDA defend itself against criticism? This question has to do with the ability of a government agency simply to refuse to undertake a serious defense of its actions, relying instead on propaganda and raw coercive power to sustain itself in the face of telling criticism.

Political Dynamics of the FDA

There is a large literature on the FDA's regulation of the drug industry. How the agency has gained and exercised greater authority is well known, although controversy continues with respect to the consequences of its drug regulation.[2] Regulation of medical devices has attracted much less attention from scholars. I maintain that one can usefully employ the same analytical framework to study the political dynamics of both FDA drug regulation and FDA device regulation.

      I view the enlargement of the FDA's powers as a process of "punctuated politics." Ordinarily the main actors—the FDA itself, certain members of Congress, organized interest groups (including self-appointed consumer advocacy groups as well as trade groups), the news media, and the public—conduct their affairs in a more or less stable situation: the FDA has fixed statutory authority, it conducts its regulation in a certain manner, and its actions have somewhat predictable consequences for others involved in the process, including the general public, which normally plays a passive role. From time to time, however, this Normal Condition changes dramatically as Congress gives the agency sweeping new authority or, less frequently, as the agency markedly alters the conduct of its regulation, including, perhaps, the way it enforces long-standing rules.

      A Normal Condition is not static. At any given time, the agency is restrained ("enveloped") by limitations inherent in existing enabling legislation and court decisions. The envelope, however, has a somewhat indefinite locus, and the agency takes enforcement actions or drafts new regulations that "push the envelope." Like any normal government bureaucracy, the FDA prefers more power to less, larger budgets to smaller, more employees to fewer. In jockeying to enhance its power and resources in a particular Normal Condition, the agency works with members of Congress, especially the chairmen and ranking minority members of pertinent committees, and their staffs; with lobbyists and representatives of organized interest groups, including "consumer advocates"; and with the news media. In the familiar phrase of political science, this activity constitutes "iron triangle politics" (or iron quadrilateral politics or iron pentagon politics as the case may be). FDA officials argue for new regulations in informal discussions with interested parties, in formal hearings, in press conferences and in news releases. The fruits of these activities appear first in the *Federal Register* and ultimately in the *Code of Federal Regulations* (CFR). Title 21 of the current CFR (revised April 1, 1992) contains eight large, densely printed volumes pertaining to the FDA. In addition, the FDA produces many letters, announcements, manuals, guidance documents, and so forth that elaborate and dilate its regulatory regime. Thus, a Normal Condition is one of creeping regulatory augmentation, as the FDA pushes its current envelope.

Occasionally the news media bring forth a shocking revelation about the danger or, less often, the ineffectiveness of a medical product. In the history of drug regulation, the classic revelations were the descriptions of unsanitary meatpacking plants in Upton Sinclair's novel *The Jungle*, which catalyzed passage of the Pure Food and Drugs Act of 1906; the Elixir Sulfanilamide tragedy, which provoked passage of the Food, Drug, and Cosmetic Act of 1938; and the thalidomide tragedy, which gave rise to the Kefauver-Harris drug amendments of 1962. In the history of device regulation, the most important shocking revelations were those related to faulty intrauterine contraceptive devices (IUDs) and cardiac pacemakers in the early 1970s, which stimulated passage of the Medical Device Amendments of 1976; fractures of the Bjork-Shiley convexo-concave heart valve, which hastened enactment of the Safe Medical Devices Act of 1990; and diseases and injuries allegedly caused by leaking silicone gel–filled breast implants, which prompted the FDA to undertake a hyperaggressive enforcement campaign in the early 1990s. A major shocking revelation produces public clamor that stimulates Congress to create new statutory authority or leads the FDA to undertake more stringent enforcement of existing regulations. This kind of change episodically creates a new Normal Condition, a bigger envelope against which the FDA pushes as before.

Figure 1 provides a schematic representation of what I have just described. The process as it occurs within a given Normal Condition is shown by the broad arrows of influence along the top and the right side of the figure. The narrow arrows of influence come into play when an episodic shocking revelation causes public clamor and thereby catalyzes the creation of broad new statutory authority or dramatically heightened enforcement activity.

The upshot of the process, so far as patients, doctors, purchasers, and providers of medical goods are concerned, is a diminished scope of discretionary individual action: what one previously could choose to do, one no longer can do; what one previously did not have to do, one now must do; and everyone must act in the same way. In short, the tendency is for varied and decentralized decision making to give way to uniform and centralized decision making, either by Congress directly or, under broad congressional authority, by the FDA in its rule making and enforcement capacities.

Figure 1

Schematic Representation of the Regulatory Process
for Drugs and Medical Devices

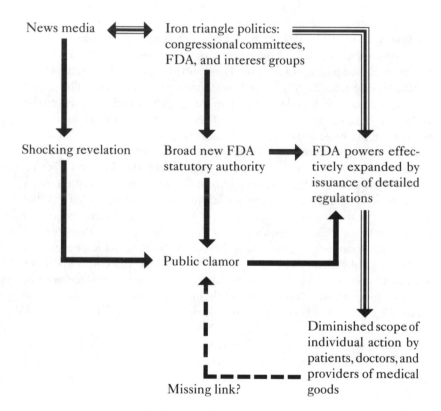

Erratum

Figure 1

Schematic Representation of the Regulatory Process for Drugs and Medical Devices

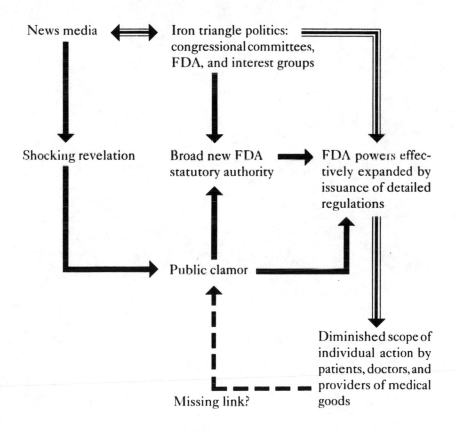

When the government deprives people of the ability to make choices affecting their own health and safety, treating them as if they were children or mental incompetents, there must exist either a deliberate official inclination to harm them or a set of strong presumptions. For purposes of debate, let us put aside the possibility of deliberate government malevolence and consider the scenario in which government officials have good intentions. The presumptions there are (1) that a government agency *knows* better than the people do what actions will promote their well-being and (2) that it will *use* this knowledge to guide its own actions so as actually to promote the people's well-being. The former is a strong assumption about the knowledge of the government agency's personnel, the latter a strong assumption about their incentives.

Central Planning

Those familiar with the long debate about socialist central planning will recognize the similarity between these assumptions and the assumptions made by those who believed socialism would promote people's economic well-being better than the free market system. The debate about socialism has been settled both in theory, as articulated by Ludwig von Mises and Friedrich Hayek, and in history, as demonstrated by the miserable experiences of the Soviet Union and the other socialist countries (see Boettke 1991). Central planning, as the saying goes, does not work. Compelled by overwhelming facts, almost everyone now recognizes this truth, and many people also understand the logic of the unworkability.

Yet, when it comes to FDA regulation, one encounters claims for what amounts to a variant of central planning that are virtually identical to the claims now recognized as discredited in relation to socialist central planning of the whole economy. But central planning does not work any better for the large sector of the U.S. economy subject to FDA regulation—about 25 percent of all consumer goods, by value—than it works for an entire economy. To succeed in making people better off, the FDA would have to solve the knowledge problem and overcome the problem of perverse incentives. The former is impossible and the latter is so unlikely as to be virtually impossible.

The major reason why FDA regulation must fail is that the people subject to it have preferences, social circumstances, and physiological attributes that vary tremendously among persons and over time and that no central planner can possibly know or deal with rationally. For the FDA, one ruling applies to all cases. Products are declared "safe and effective" or not. A product is permitted to be sold to everybody or to nobody. These dichotomies mock the heterogeneities of actual life. In reality, a product that is too risky for one person is acceptable to another; only the users can

say (see Eraker and Sox 1981). In reality, a drug or device that is not
effective for one person is quite effective for another; individuals vary
widely, for example, in their responses to drugs. In reality, a product's
adverse side effects may differ enormously from one user to another. But
in the FDA's world, everything is black or white. The FDA makes the old
Soviet Gosplan look like a dealer in nuance.

Even if the FDA could know the infinitely varied and changeable
information it would require to promote the public interest, one would be
naive to suppose that it would act on the basis of that information. What
incentive would its personnel have to do so? Do people become angels
simply by signing on with the agency? Do officials put aside their interest
in job security when they work for the FDA? Do we have any reason to
suppose that the people who work for the FDA are any more public spirited
than those who work for the Bureau of Land Management, the Export-
Import Bank, or the Postal Service?

Sad to say, the consequence of empowering the FDA to rule over
people in matters of drugs, devices, and other medical goods is, within the
affected domain, the same as the consequence of adopting socialist central
planning for the whole economy: people in general are made worse off; the
only ones who systematically benefit are those who wield the powers—in
this case, selected members of Congress and the bureaucrats themselves,
along with a handful of lawyers, consultants, "consumerists," and others
who feed off the regulatory regime regardless of its overall effects on the
public. As one commentator on FDA drug regulation has put it, "The
result is impressive: expensive drugs, lack of innovation, and no improvement in drug safety" (Beckner 1993). Thanks to the FDA, hundreds of
thousands of Americans have died prematurely and far more have suffered
unnecessarily.[3] Multitudes have been denied opportunities to assume a
risk they considered worth bearing, given the expected benefits. With a
paternalistic "father" like the FDA, orphanhood would be a blessing.

In actuality the whole apparatus—the drug and device laws and
the operations of the agency authorized to enforce them—is a sham, a cruel
hoax. Yet many Americans are startled by this observation and refuse to
accept even the possibility of its truth. In opinion polls, the FDA "seems
generally perceived as not only performing an important function but as
doing it well."[4] Among those who have investigated the relevant evidence
carefully and in detail, however, acceptance of the truth comes far more
readily. The problem for most citizens is that they simply have taken for
granted that the FDA can and does protect them from harm and improve
their well-being. They accept this notion because they have been told
repeatedly by the authorities that it is so, and no one has ever given them
good reasons to doubt it.

The Official Rationale

When criticized, the FDA typically employs one of two tactics: most often it just ignores the criticism; less often it simply denies the critic's claims. The denials are customarily not reasoned and documented but broad and sweeping denials: take it or leave it. For example, in testimony before a congressional committee (quoted in Seidman 1977) an FDA official said:

> The allegation has been made that the cost to our society to prevent a thalidomide-type tragedy far exceeds the benefits of a regulatory system developed to prevent such a tragedy. We disagree. We believe that benefits which accrue to society because of our regulatory system are worth the cost and far outweigh any risks.

This statement, which expresses the agency's standard line, is remarkable in at least five ways.

First, it cites the most notorious medical tragedy of modern times to illustrate what, presumably, FDA regulation routinely prevents. The presumption is indefensible. Except in a freakishly unlikely case, one may not reasonably assume that an unregulated manufacturer would sell a medical good giving rise to a "thalidomide-type tragedy." Besides their ethics, manufacturers have good financial reasons, including product liability judgments and loss of consumer confidence, to be careful about what they place on the market. Moreover, manufacturers have learned a great deal about potential problems and how to avoid them since a German company began selling thalidomide in the 1950s. Science and technology have come a long way in the past 40 years.

Second, the statement stands alone, without any attempt to demonstrate that the lives saved and the suffering prevented exceed the lives lost and the suffering endured as a result of FDA regulation. It is merely a naked declaration, which the audience presumably should accept because it emanates from the official "experts." But it is almost certainly the case that whatever the scientific issue, greater expertise always exists outside the agency.[5] Indeed, part of the problem at the FDA—though it is not a fundamental part of the problem—is that its personnel often lack state-of-the-art understanding of the scientific and technological matters subject to their regulation.

Third, the statement refers to the benefits and costs of the regulation as if they were experienced by society at large rather than by specific individuals, who differ enormously in their personal valuation of costs and benefits and in their willingness to bear risk. It rests on the unspoken assumption that a single rule should apply in all cases, disregarding the actual heterogeneity of people's preferences, social circumstances, and medical conditions.

Fourth, the statement confidently declares "*we* disagree" and "*we* believe" while describing the balance of benefits and costs experienced by others. But only specific individuals can possibly know whether the benefits *to them* outweigh the costs *to them*. Neither the benefits nor the costs can be objectively assessed by third parties; nor can the benefits and costs experienced by many individuals be aggregated into total or "social" valuations and thereby be made comparable. There is no common unit of account in which the aggregation may be made. Who knows how to measure the depth of one person's fear, the breadth of another's relief?

Finally, the statement presumes an answer—the wrong answer— to the question posed by AIDS activist and FDA critic Martin Delaney: "Who should decide which risks are acceptable—the bureaucracy in Washington or the patient whose life is on the line?" At bottom, this is a moral question, and it must be said that in matters of morals, the FDA deserves a failing grade, because it presumes to exercise control over people's lives that cannot possibly be justified unless one views people as having no more rights than the sheep in a flock (see Machan 1994).

After the FDA received uncharacteristic criticism on a major television network broadcast—ABC's *20/20* program of August 12, 1994— Susan Alpert, director of the Office of Device Evaluation in the FDA's Center for Devices and Radiological Health, responded that clinicians could not perform acceptably without the agency's regulation. In her view, FDA makes

> the benefits/risk assessment…on the technology, on the intervention, in the global sense, and then each clinician makes that benefit/risk assessment again knowing how the product performs and then takes that down to the patient level. We think both levels are still important. …[Y]ou need to make two separate kinds of decisions, the decision of benefit/risk in the larger community, and then the individual benefit/risk. And we don't see, at this point in time, how the individual clinician making the decision would provide that larger arena of benefit/risk.[6]

This statement reveals fundamental misconceptions—and a determination to make those misconceptions the foundation for coercive government policy. It is a fallacy of reification to suppose that *anyone* can weigh benefits against risks for "the larger community." The expected benefits of medical goods and the associated costs of risk bearing are not experienced by the community at large; they exist solely in the minds of distinct individuals, whose evaluations do not have a common measure.

Nor are we dealing with what economists call a "public good," which, if created to any degree at all, is necessarily created to that same degree for everyone. Quite the contrary is the case. An individual who judges the use of a certain type of medical good desirable may use it without affecting in any way the extent to which other individuals may use or refrain from using the same type of good, and without affecting the desirability of their deciding one way or the other. The goods regulated by FDA—foods, drugs, devices, and dietary supplements—are unquestionably "private goods" in the economist's sense of the term. And the performance of a social benefit/cost assessment would be inappropriate even if such an assessment could be conducted in a meaningful way.[7]

FDA officials are content to defend their policies with raw assertions, expressing *ex parte* judgments and referring to meaningless collectivist concepts. Obviously, they feel no obligation to justify the agency's actions in an intellectually serious way. They settle for wielding power.

Most of all, the FDA and its congressional and media supporters rely on people's ignorance and inclination to assume that *of course* the government would not do anything harmful or misguided in its regulation of drugs and medical devices.

Ideology helps the FDA cause, too. People who know little or nothing about the pertinent facts fill the gaps with ideological assumptions. Many people assume that businesses try to profit from the sale of dangerous products and therefore must be strictly regulated by government. Many people assume that elected officials take care to guard the public interest, that democratically elected officials know what kind of law is in the public interest and dedicate themselves to enacting it. Many people assume that regulators are disinterested experts who care only about public health and safety and not about their own positions, power, and perks, that FDA officials in particular are dedicated public servants whose failings occur only because Congress will not provide them sufficient funds to do what should be done. Such ideological assumptions are hazardous to our health.[8]

Fortunately, we can get beyond assumptions, conjectures, and ideological predilections; we can examine the facts and the findings and conclusions of independent authorities. As we do so, in the chapters that follow, we shall see that the facts conform to patterns, and that the actions of Congress and the FDA are far from random. Indeed they are quite systematic. So these studies provide more than a tragic account of what has happened in the past. They serve also as a warning of what awaits us if, like trusting children, we continue to submit to the paternalism of the FDA, an agency whose officials utter reassuring words while augmenting our suffering and hastening our demise.

Notes

1. Nobel 1993, 5. Dr. Nobel is the president of ECRI (originally the Emergency Care Research Institute), an organization "engaged in technology assessment, product evaluation, medical device accident and forensic investigation, user education, and related issues." ECRI is completely independent of both government and industry and enjoys the highest reputation for technical competence. Its address is 5200 Butler Pike, Plymouth Meeting, PA, 19462.

2. Standard references include Temin 1980 and Grabowski and Vernon 1983. More recent appraisals include Siegel and Roberts 1991, Ward 1992, Beckner 1993, and Ronald W. Hansen's chapter in this book.

3. Evidence underlying this conclusion appears in the chapters that follow.

4. Lasagna 1989, 322. Lasagna adds, "Perception and reality are, to be sure, not the same, and it is disquieting to learn that many Americans believe that the FDA actually tests the safety and efficacy of new drugs before they are approved for sale." In fact, the manufacturers perform the tests.

5. Observes Dr. Lasagna, "The FDA considers itself to contain the 'experts.'" See Lasagna 1989, 336.

6. Alpert's statement to the Utah International Medical Device Congress, Salt Lake City, August 18, 1994, as quoted in "'Safety Only' Device Evaluation" 1994, 10.

7. Social cost/benefit assessments are meaningless in any event. See Buchanan 1979, 60–61, 15152; and Formaini 1990, 39–65.

8. An excellent introductory antidote to such mistaken assumptions is Mitchell and Simmons 1994.

References

Beckner, C. Frederick, III. 1993. "The FDA's War on Drugs." *Georgetown Law Journal* 82 (December): 529–62

Boettke, Peter J. 1991. "The Austrian Critique and the Demise of Socialism: The Soviet Case." In *Austrian Economics: Perspectives on the Past and Prospects for the Future,* ed. Richard M. Ebeling, pp. 181–231. Hillsdale, Mich.: Hillsdale College Press.

Buchanan, James M. 1979. *What Should Economists Do?* Indianapolis: Liberty Press.

Eraker, Stephen A., and Harold C. Sox. 1981. "Assessment of Patients' Preferences for Therapeutic Outcomes." *Medical Decision Making* 1: 29–39.

Formaini, Robert. 1990. *The Myth of Scientific Public Policy.* New Brunswick, N.J.: Transaction Publishers.

Grabowski, Henry G., and John M. Vernon. 1983. *The Regulation of Pharmaceuticals: Balancing the Benefits and Risks.* Washington, D.C.: American Enterprise Institute for Public Policy Research.

Kwitny, Jonathan. 1992. *Acceptable Risks.* New York: Poseidon Press.

Lasagna, Louis. 1989. "Congress, the FDA, and New Drug Development: Before and After 1962." *Perspectives in Biology and Medicine* 32 (Spring).

Machan, Tibor. 1994. *Private Rights and Public Illusions.* An Independent Institute book. New Brunswick, N.J.: Transaction Publishers.

Mitchell, William C., and Randy T. Simmons. 1994. *Beyond Politics: Markets, Welfare, and the Failure of Bureaucracy.* An Independent Institute book. Boulder, Colo.: Westview Press.

Nobel, Joel J. 1993. Draft of 1993 address to Utah Biomedical Congress.

Page, Jim. 1992. "Can You Trust Your FDA?" *Journal of Emergency Medical Services* 17 (August).

"'Safety Only' Device Evaluation Inconsistent with Cost-Containment." 1994. *Medical Devices, Diagnostics & Instrumentation*, August 29.

Seidman, David. 1977. "The Politics of Policy Analysis." *Regulation* (July/ August).

Siegel, Joanna E., and Marc J. Roberts. 1991. "Reforming FDA Policy: Lessons from the AIDS Experience." *Regulation* 14 (Fall): 71–77.

Temin, Peter. 1980. *Taking Your Medicine: Drug Regulation in the United States.* Cambridge: Harvard University Press.

Ward, Michael R. 1992. "Drug Approval Overregulation." *Regulation* 15 (Fall): 47–53.

2

FDA Regulation of the Pharmaceutical Industry

Ronald W. Hansen

In the recent debates over health care reform, the pharmaceutical industry has been the subject of much criticism. Although pharmaceuticals represent only 8 percent of total health care expenditures, pharmaceutical firms represent some of the largest individual suppliers of health products. Official reports indicating that pharmaceutical prices rose faster than most other health care prices during the 1980s and recent introductions of new products at prices that seem high by historical standards have drawn additional attention to prices and profits in the industry. Despite the growth of HMOs (Health Maintenance Organizations) and other comprehensive health plans, outpatient pharmaceuticals remain one of the major health care costs paid directly by patients. Even though pharmaceuticals are a relatively minor part of the total expenditures on health care, they often represent the single largest direct expenditure for individuals. It is not surprising, therefore, that the pharmaceutical industry has been singled out as a potential source of cost savings through either price controls or formulary restrictions.

Even without major health care reform legislation from Congress, the pharmaceutical marketplace, like many other segments of the health care sector, is undergoing major changes. Despite the best efforts of some groups to hold back the tide, these marketplace changes will continue to have a major impact on the conduct and performance of the pharmaceutical industry. The locus of decision making in pharmaceutical markets has

13

changed. While physicians continue to play a key role in selecting pharmaceuticals for their patients, pharmaceutical utilization decisions are increasingly being influenced by health care administrators. HMOs and other plans with pharmaceutical reimbursements often employ formularies that restrict the choice of pharmaceuticals, or have provisions that encourage the utilization of less expensive or generic products. Several firms have faced the choice of either giving an HMO deep discounts or dealing with the prospect of being excluded from the formulary. These changes have shifted the focus of pharmaceutical marketing from an almost exclusive focus on medical effectiveness to more consideration of cost effectiveness. Thus, the existing and projected changes in the health care marketplace will exert considerable influence on the research and development investment decisions by pharmaceutical firms.

In the midst of all the changes in the pharmaceutical marketplace, firms must also be concerned about the regulatory environment which affects their ability to generate new products for the evolving marketplace. Pharmaceutical research and development remains one of the most heavily regulated industrial activities. All pharmaceuticals must be approved by the FDA prior to marketing. The FDA's influence extends to the research and development process leading up to a marketing approval as well as to the manufacturing of the product and the marketing claims that the firms can make. The FDA policies determine which potential technologies are available, affect the cost of developing those technologies, and at least indirectly influence the research areas pursued by the pharmaceutical industry.

Regulation of Pharmaceutical Products

The federal government's role in regulating the pharmaceutical industry began with the 1906 Pure Food and Drugs Act. Adulteration of food was the primary focus of the bill, and the Department of Agriculture was responsible for enforcing the provisions of the Act. Of the first 1000 notices of judgment issued by the Department's Bureau of Chemistry prior to August 1911, over three-quarters were for food violations (Wardell and Lasagna 1975). The Act focused on proper labeling, not advertising. In 1911 the Supreme Court ruled that therapeutic claims were not covered by the provisions prohibiting false and misleading claims. False and fraudulent claims in patent medicine were banned by the tougher Sherley Amendment in 1912. Even with this act the court subsequently ruled that, if the seller believed his therapeutic claims, there was no case of fraud, thus greatly limiting the government control of drugs.

Prior to the 1930s most of the drugs were derived from plant materials. The Department of Agriculture's concern was primarily with the quality of the derived product and its labeling. The 1930s witnessed the development of the sulfa drugs. After the Elixir Sulfanilamide tragedy in 1937, the Food, Drug, and Cosmetic Act of 1938 was passed; it required that firms demonstrate to the FDA that their products were safe prior to marketing them.

The wonder drugs of the early post–World War II period sparked the growth of the modern pharmaceutical industry, complete with an emphasis on research, development, and promotion of new products. This resulted in concern about controlling the promotion and usage of these more powerful drugs. The Humphrey-Durham amendment in 1951 codified the distinction between prescription-only and nonprescription drugs.

As the modern pharmaceutical industry continued to expand, so did the criticism of the industry. In December 1959, Senator Estes Kefauver, chair of the Subcommittee on Antitrust and Monopoly, opened hearings on the drug industry that extended over 26 months. In the course of these hearings, critics claimed that firms engaged in excessive and unsubstantiated promotion, earned excessive profits, and spent too much on "me-too" innovation. The massive legislation that grew out of these hearings nearly died in Congress. However, the occurrence of the thalidomide tragedy focused attention on the potential for harm from the new pharmaceuticals and revived interest in strengthening the regulation of the pharmaceutical industry. Although many of Kefauver's proposals were shelved, Congress unanimously passed the revised Kefauver-Harris bill in 1962 (Lasagna 1989).

The legislation, which is referred to as the 1962 Amendments to the Food, Drug, and Cosmetic Act, is a major milestone in the history of pharmaceutical regulation. One principal feature of the act was the requirement that firms wait for FDA approval prior to marketing. (The previous law required them to submit evidence of safety to the FDA; then they could begin marketing if the FDA did not object.) Another central feature was the efficacy requirement, which required firms to demonstrate that their product was efficacious for all the claimed indications. Although we often use the language that a product is approved for marketing, in fact it is approved only for sale for specific claims. If firms wish to broaden their claimed indications, they must file a supplemental new drug application (NDA) and submit evidence to support these claims.

Simultaneously with the new amendments, the FDA began regulating clinical trials. Prior to testing new drug candidates in humans, firms must file an IND (investigational new drug) exemption. To obtain approval of an IND, firms must submit evidence of the drug candidate's safety. Since most new drug candidates are new chemical entities (NCEs) that have not been used by humans, this evidence consists largely of data from animal trials. The firm must also submit its clinical testing protocols, including evidence that only human subjects who give informed consent will be test subjects.

Through this mechanism, which is designed to protect human subjects, and its GLP (good laboratory practices) regulations, the FDA exerts considerable control over the conduct of clinical trials. This is in sharp contrast to the pre-1962 period, in which FDA involvement usually began when the firm submitted its application to market a product.

The clinical trial stage is usually described as occurring in three phases, progressing from relatively short-term trials in Phase I, which are usually designed to show safety in healthy volunteers, to initial trials in patients in Phase II, and finally to the large-scale clinical trials in Phase III, which are designed to demonstrate efficacy as well as to provide further evidence of safety. When the firm gathers evidence it deems to be sufficient to demonstrate safety and efficacy, it files a new drug application (NDA) with the FDA. On average, this occurs approximately six years after the beginning of clinical trials. The FDA then reviews the NDA; approval typically requires 30 months. Depending on the nature of the drug candidate, the clinical trials may extend into the NDA review phase.

Regulation does not end with the approval of an NDA. The GMP (good manufacturing practices) regulations provide standards for the manufacture of products. The FDA also monitors the promotional efforts of pharmaceutical firms. Firms can make only claims about their product which have been approved by the FDA, and they are also required to supply information on possible adverse effects. In some cases, the pharmaceutical firm and the FDA spend a lot of effort negotiating the language that can be used in promotional efforts.

The 1984 Drug Price Competition and Patent Term Restoration Act clarified the requirements for firms to manufacture generic versions of products whose patents had expired while simultaneously providing for some extension of patents based on regulatory review times. Although this act had little effect on the manner in which new pharmaceuticals were regulated, it has had a major impact on the pharmaceutical marketplace and on the FDA's workload. Applications for generic approvals virtually overwhelmed the FDA staff and resulted in serious questions about the FDA's ability to conduct its other functions. This was in part responsible for the initiation of an NDA filing fee, which is supposed to provide supplemental funding for FDA review of NCE NDAs.

Lately there has been considerable concern about unapproved uses of pharmaceuticals and the possible role of firms in promoting these uses. As noted earlier, when the FDA approves a new pharmaceutical, it specifies the claimed uses that are approved. Often a pharmaceutical product may have other potential uses. In some cases the firm may have been aware of the potential uses during the clinical trial stage, but either chose not to invest the additional resources necessary to demonstrate those uses or was unable to obtain FDA approval for those claims. Other times these uses are discovered only after the product has been approved. Firms may choose to conduct additional clinical trials and file a supplemental NDA to broaden the claimed uses. If the patent has expired, or is about to expire, the firm may have little incentive to finance these additional tests. (It does receive three years exclusivity for marketing these claims, which often is hard to monitor or enforce.) Physicians often become aware of these unapproved uses either through articles in medical journals or through less formal sources. The FDA cannot prevent physicians from prescribing drugs for unapproved uses; however, liability concerns or managed health care oversight may prevent physicians from doing so. At the FDA, concern has arisen about the role of pharmaceutical firms in sponsoring clinical trials on additional uses (but not filing a supplemental NDA) and disseminating published articles.

Although the statutory authority has remained relatively unchanged, there is a constant evolution of FDA-initiated regulation of the development, manufacturing, and distribution of drugs and medical devices. Some of these changes are codified in specific regulations; others are more subtle changes in interpretations. Since many changes occur gradually, it is often hard to measure their impact.

Costs and Benefits of Regulation in an Ideal Environment

In the best of all worlds there are several benefits and costs that might result from the regulation of the pharmaceutical industry by the FDA. The principal benefit claimed is the elimination of unsafe and ineffective drugs, thereby reducing the harmful effects on patients either directly from unsafe drugs or indirectly from delaying proper therapy as the result of using an ineffective drug. Control over the claims that companies could make for their products would reduce the need for physicians to verify independently the claims made for products that they prescribed, thus reducing information costs. To the extent that the administration of the regulations discouraged me-too research, research would be directed to more innovative projects.

Against these benefits, even strong proponents of regulation recognize that there are some additional costs. Achieving the desired proof of safety and effectiveness may require more testing than the firms would voluntarily conduct and hence increase development costs. How great this effect might be depends not only on the stringency of the FDA regulations but also on the nature of liability laws and the importance of reputation effects in the marketing of products.

One source of a measured increase in the average cost of developing approved new drugs is the elimination of unsafe or ineffective drugs from the list of approved drugs used to calculate the average. If this were the only source of increased average cost, then there should not be much concern about increased average development cost. To the extent that FDA regulations truly increased the cost of developing safe and effective drugs, then the regulations will reduce research and development (R&D) efforts. In particular, these increased costs will endanger the development of drugs for small therapeutic markets. The market may be small because the underlying disease is rare or because only a small number of people do not respond satisfactorily to the existing therapies. This gave rise to concern over the so-called orphan drugs, drug candidates that could not find a sponsor willing to conduct the clinical trials necessary to obtain FDA approval. The 1984 Orphan Drug Act provided special tax relief and/or exclusive marketing rights to companies that develop orphan drugs.

To the extent that the regulations have discouraged the development of me-too products, there are costs that are often overlooked by those who view such research as wasteful. First, a relatively minor change in a drug's composition may provide a major improvement in therapy or a reduction in side effects. It may also provide an alternative therapy for those patients who do not respond to or cannot tolerate the first drug in the class. The me-too products also provide market competition for the initial innovator. Many firms are discovering that the pharmaceutical marketplace is increasingly being influenced by price-sensitive managed health care providers and that the existence of me-too products has had a depressing effect on their prices and sales. Those who argue for less me-too research should not simultaneously deplore the lack of competition in the pharmaceutical marketplace.

Critics of FDA Regulation

There have been a large number of critics of the FDA's regulation of the pharmaceutical industry. The principal criticisms fall into three main categories: excessively long approval times, excessive costs, and improper decisions.

Dr. William Wardell (1973a) published a study that compared availability of new pharmaceuticals in Great Britain and the United States for the decade ending in 1971. The study revealed that not only were more drugs exclusively available in Great Britain, but for products introduced in both countries, drug approval averaged two years later in the United States. This phenomenon, which became known as the "drug lag," has been studied by other researchers using different time periods and countries for comparisons. A study by Kaitin, Mattison, et al. (1989), for the period 1977 through 1987, demonstrated that the drug lag continued to average about two years. These drug lag studies have been used as benchmarks for measuring performance of regulatory agencies.

The significance of a drug lag extends beyond its measurement of regulatory performance. On average, therapies are not available to patients in the United States until two years after they are in use in Great Britain. The significance of this unavailability depends on the particular drug therapy as well as the therapeutic alternatives available in each country. Kaitin et al. note that of drugs classified by the FDA as representing important therapeutic gains (class 1-A), four times as many were first introduced in the United Kingdom. However, as they note, determining the overall therapeutic significance is very difficult.

Several studies have investigated the time required to obtain approval to market pharmaceuticals. For studies of the drug approval process in the United States, typically three milestones are used: the date of IND approval (or alternatively, the date of the start of clinical trials), the date of NDA filing, and the date of NDA approval by the FDA. The period from IND approval to NDA filing is often referred to as the clinical development or IND phase, the time from NDA filing to NDA approval as the regulatory review or NDA phase, and the total time from IND approval to NDA approval as the total regulatory phase. The Center for the Study of Drug Development has published a series of papers tracking the drug development process (DiMasi, Bryant, and Lasagna 1991; Kaitin, Manocchia, et al. 1994; Mattison et al. 1988). The most frequently used data series involves self-originated new chemical entities (NCEs) of U.S. companies. Their studies demonstrate that there has been a rather steady increase in overall development times. Even if the decade of the 1960s is ignored (due to start-up effects in the data series), published studies reveal a significant increase in time required to obtain marketing approval from around six years in the early 1970s to more than eight years currently. There have been increases in both the IND and the NDA phases.

One unintended consequence of the lengthening regulatory period was the reduction of effective patent life (defined as the time between approval to market and the expiration of the product patent). Eisman and Wardell (1987) demonstrated that for new drugs approved in the early 1980s, the effective patent life had declined to less than 10 years. Concern about this effect of the lengthening regulatory process resulted in legislation to provide extensions of pharmaceutical patents for up to five extra years, provided that the total effective patent life shall not exceed fourteen years. While these provisions in the Drug Price Competition and Patent Term Restoration Act of 1984 provide some relief to pharmaceutical firms, for the longer regulatory period, as Grabowski, Vernon, and Thomas (1978) and others have pointed out, a one-year reduction in regulatory time is of much more value than a one-year extension of a patent.

In addition to these general studies, some critics focus on particu-
lar drugs or drug categories. The most dramatic recent examples are
provided by those concerned with the development of AIDS therapies.
Their vocal criticisms of the FDA have led to a variety of policy changes.
In October 1988, the FDA issued its Interim Rule on Procedures for Drugs
Intended to Treat Life-Threatening and Severely Debilitating Illness,
designed to speed the development and approval of new therapies to treat
AIDS and other life-threatening diseases. In particular, it contains provisions designed to provide for greater preapproval use of therapies through
treatment INDs and reduced premarketing studies in exchange for expanded postmarketing studies. These procedures are similar to those that
the FDA followed on a more ad hoc basis in approving AZT for AIDS
treatment and L-Dopa for Parkinson's disease (Kaitin 1991).

The rising cost of developing new pharmaceuticals has been
blamed in part on excessive FDA regulations. When I conducted my first
study of the cost of developing NCEs as pharmaceuticals, based on a
sample of NCEs that were first tested in humans between 1963 and 1975,
my estimate that the average cost was $54 million (1977 dollars) contrasted
sharply with the previously generally accepted number ($20 million) and
pre-1962 estimates of $6 million (Hansen 1979). In a study of a more recent
period (drug candidates that entered clinical trials between 1970 and 1982),
Joe DiMasi, Henry Grabowski, Lou Lasagna, and I (1991) estimated the
average cost to be $231 million (1987 dollars). Congress's Office of
Technology Assessment (OTA) estimated the development cost using the
same data but applying a higher cost of capital, which ranged from 14
percent for early development periods to 10 percent for the later stages
(U.S. Congress 1993). Their estimate of R&D costs was $359 million (1990
dollars). All three of the studies were capitalized pretax estimates.

The increase between the Hansen study and the later studies is
due partly to inflation (in 1987 dollars the earlier estimate would be $100
million) and partly to the use of an 8 percent rather than the 9 percent cost
of capital in DiMasi et al. or the sliding scale used in the OTA study.
Correcting for these differences in parameters, the studies indicate that
real development costs have doubled in roughly ten years. The DiMasi et
al. study further revealed that the cost escalation is likely to continue. The
average cost of testing for the drugs in the latter half of the sample was
roughly double that for those in the first half.

These studies measure the cost of developing new pharmaceuticals but do not try to separately identify sources of cost increases. Changes
in acceptable standards of evidence, differences in therapeutic areas
(chronic conditions require more testing), and extra studies for marketing
purposes are all offered as explanations. However, the rising cost and other
evidence, some of which is anecdotal, points to regulation as one of the

major causes of increased development cost. Critics also note that despite large increases in the funds spent on R&D, the number of drugs approved annually dropped after 1962 and has remained relatively stable in the low twenties.

Wrong Decisions

One of the problems for the FDA is that decisions they make based on evidence from clinical trials may later prove to be incorrect. In part this is due to the occurrence of rare effects that may not appear in the clinical trial data or effects that become apparent only after prolonged exposure or the passage of time. Should the FDA approve a drug that later is shown to have serious side effects, the FDA can be assured of criticism. Moreover, with hindsight some may be able to point to clues in the clinical data that should have indicated the presence of this negative effect.

Less visible are the effects of delaying or failing to approve a useful new drug. Individuals who may benefit from new therapies are denied access to products that may extend or improve their lives. Some people travel abroad to obtain new therapies, but most are unaware of improved therapies prior to FDA approval. Even if the drug is ultimately approved, some users are effectively denied access.

What is the optimum error rate? Attempts to reduce errors of the first type may involve increases in the numbers of test subjects, longer testing times, and increased data collection per subject. All these will add to the cost of developing drugs and hence may result in decisions not to pursue drug candidates, some of which may have very beneficial properties. Moreover, to the extent that these measures add to the total length of time required to develop a drug, they add to the second type of error, effectively denying some patients access to a useful therapy. With consideration to the relative costs of type one and type two errors (which will vary by product), one would recommend that different standards be applied across drugs. At present there are differences in testing protocols, many of which do vary across drug classes. An interesting question, but one which requires medical expertise, is how well these requirements correlate with minimizing the cost of type one and two errors.

Inherent Problems in Regulating the Safety of Medical Technologies

One fundamental problem in regulating the safety of medical technologies is defining safety. Pharmaceuticals and many other medical technologies are designed to treat conditions that are "unsafe." One needs to be concerned not only with the inherent safety of the medical technology, but also with the risk of the underlying disease. In an ideal setting, one should try to reduce total risk by balancing the disease and medical technology risks.

Balancing technology and disease risks is difficult to do in a one-size-fits-all system. Individuals differ in their willingness to accept treatment risks versus disease risks. Some individuals may find the disease so intolerable that they would accept a 50-50 chance of cure versus death, whereas others with identical disease conditions would submit to the therapy only if the potential for an adverse outcome were less than 2 percent. In theory, we could have the FDA act as an information certifying agency and allow doctors and patients to decide whether the risk of the drug is preferable to the risk of the disease. In practice, we recognize that the risk information can be difficult to interpret and that the FDA eliminates some of the choices by not approving them for market. Implicitly we have a lower level of product risk below which the FDA will not allow the product to be marketed. This eliminates products that some segments of the market might find useful. Empirically it is an open question as to whether the cost of these lost uses exceeds the additional cost from the extra decision making and potentially wrong choices.

There are institutional biases in the safety assessment process. As noted earlier, the errors that can be made are (1) approving what turns out to be a bad drug and (2) denial or delay in approving a useful drug. It has often been noted that the system neither rewards speedy approvals of useful new drugs nor punishes the second error. However, it does punish approvals of drugs that turn out to be undesirable. Thus, institutionally there is a bias in favor of slow decision and high thresholds of safety. This bias is not due to bad regulators. Rather, it is a product of the incentive system facing the regulatory agency.

Inherent in the institutional problem are problems of information and risk perception. On the information side, the public at large, and even many physicians, are basically unaware of what is in the system. Only after the drug is approved or nears approval is there likely to be widespread awareness of the activity of the drug. Thus, there is little pressure to speed approval. The other problem is rooted in risk perception. Consider a drug that is an improvement in an area where there are already some therapies. Even if the new drug reduces mortality from 30 to 20 percent, usually one cannot identify the 10 percent who would not have survived without the new therapy. But if the drug is shown to be responsible for killing a specific individual, then that loss becomes much more identifiable than all the survivors. The public and Congress will respond to the identifiable risks, which will receive disproportionate emphasis. Even if the regulators were to attempt to incorporate both the observed and the unobserved risks, the public and congressional pressures would be immense enough to force a behavior biased toward the observed. In the case of pharmaceutical regulation, the effect will be biased against new introductions.

As noted earlier, pharmaceuticals also must be shown to be effective. The proof of efficacy poses a different problem. Ultimately we are interested in the health of individuals. In predicting future health status, we often use surrogate measures such as blood pressure and cholesterol levels. High levels of either of these markers is associated with a higher risk of coronary disease. For drugs designed to lower blood pressure or cholesterol levels, is it sufficient to demonstrate that they do lower these levels, or is it necessary to further demonstrate that this will result in a lower risk of heart disease? Some independent studies indicate that lowering these levels may not be sufficient to reduce heart disease. Should we then require that firms do longer-term studies, say an additional 5 to 15 years, to demonstrate that their drug indeed reduces mortality and morbidity, or are the surrogate markers sufficient? The answers to questions such as these have major implications for the cost of developing drugs and for the timing of new therapeutic introductions.

Regulatory Reforms

There are several suggestions for regulatory reforms that will, if approved, encourage the development of new medical technologies.

Regulatory reforms were recently addressed by then Vice President Quayle's Competitiveness Council and the Lasagna Committee. The Competitiveness Council, in focusing on ways to make the U.S. pharmaceutical industry more competitive in world markets, suggested several reforms in the FDA regulatory process. Chief among the recommendations was to reduce the premarketing tests and substitute more postmarketing studies, holding the FDA responsible for faster review times, and harmonization of U.S. regulations and data requirements with foreign, particularly European, regulatory authorities.

Eliminating Phase III and relying on expanded postmarketing surveillance is a particularly attractive option for pharmaceuticals designed to treat life-threatening illnesses for which there are no suitable therapies. As noted earlier, the FDA has already taken steps in this direction. Applying the same procedure to other pharmaceutical products also has the potential for earlier introduction of improved therapies. The procedure may also lower the expected development costs and further enhance pharmaceutical innovation. There is the possibility that the expected savings may be eroded by Phase II creep, that is, the Phase II trials may expand and partially offset the savings resulting from the elimination of Phase III.

A more serious danger to this proposed reform lies in the possibility of a drug marketed under this procedure being found to have serious adverse effects after being marketed. Depending on the seriousness of the adverse effects, this may cause the whole system to collapse back to its current structure. It should be noted that several years ago many AIDS activists were strong proponents of eliminating Phase III trails in order to obtain speedier access to promising AIDS therapies. As noted earlier, the FDA did enact procedures to provide early release of AIDS drugs. Now some of these activists are concerned about the side effects of drugs released early and have proposed a return to earlier approval standards.

The proposal to harmonize our drug regulations with those of the European community seems particularly attractive on the surface. It certainly should make the life of the regulatory affairs staff in a pharmaceutical company much easier. They potentially could file the same application in all their major markets, rather than tailor each to the requirements of individual agencies. There is, however, a danger lurking in this proposal that may in the longer term make it much harder or more costly to obtain marketing approval.

As noted earlier, one event that focused attention on the performance of the FDA was the publication of the drug lag studies. These studies effectively benchmarked U.S. approval times to those in the United Kingdom. If the major regulatory agencies harmonize the regulatory process, particularly if the systems effectively collapse into a single agency, there will be no benchmark for comparison. Should the super-agency prove to be slower in decision making or more conservative in the approval process, it will be harder to determine what innovative technologies are being delayed or lost. Although the word harmonization puts a very positive cast on this proposal, perhaps we should better think of it as regulatory monopoly.

The FDA in the New Health Care Market

This chapter began with the observation that the pharmaceutical marketplace is in the process of major changes. In particular, many of the industry's customers are interested in cost effectiveness as well as medical effectiveness. How do FDA regulations fit in this new environment?

The FDA has long regarded itself as focused on safety and medical effectiveness, not price. To be acceptable, a new pharmaceutical must be at least as safe and effective as existing products and hopefully superior in one dimension. To a large extent, its criteria for acceptability have evolved into relative safety and relative effectiveness. There does not appear to be room for a product that is almost as safe as or almost as effective as existing products but cheaper. If there are Cadillacs on the market, then Chevrolets are not approvable.

The FDA's criteria fit relatively well with firms' objectives when the marketplace focused on improved medical effectiveness. However, the emerging concern with cost effectiveness is potentially at odds with the FDA's approval criteria. The purchasers of pharmaceuticals may be willing to trade away some medical effectiveness to obtain cost savings. In markets where the existing technologies are relatively expensive, market forces could encourage firms to devote R&D to developing less expensive technology even if it were slightly inferior in terms of safety or efficacy. However, these technologies may not be approvable by the FDA using past criteria.

This poses a major dilemma for regulatory policy. Should cost effectiveness be part of the criteria? I suspect that if you polled pharmaceutical industry leaders and FDA officials, the answer would be a resounding "no." There are major unresolved methodological issues in cost effectiveness analysis in health care. In particular there is no consensus on how one should value changes in health. Defining cost effectiveness has some of the same characteristics as defining safety noted previously. A product may be cost effective in some situations but not in others. This may depend on patients' other medical conditions, their preferences or parameters such as age, income, etc. Should we try to define cost effectiveness without specifying the context or would the FDA need to specify conditions in which a product is approvable?

R&D managers are right to be concerned that a cost effectiveness mandate would add one more degree of uncertainty to the approval process. The FDA has not had to develop expertise in this area. Adding this as a criterion would require a significant change in personnel and the decision process.

It may be difficult to find individuals willing to advocate that R&D be invested in developing medical technologies that are therapeutically inferior to existing technologies. But if cost limits access to the first-line technologies, then a compelling case could be made for developing somewhat inferior technologies if this broadens access. If this view is accepted, then the next challenge will be to make the FDA process consistent with accepting less effective or less safe technologies. It is a view that runs counter to the prevailing practice.

References

DiMasi, J. A., N. R. Bryant, and L. Lasagna. 1991. "New Drug Development in the United States from 1963 to 1990." *Clinical Pharmacology and Therapeutics* 50 (5): 471–86.

DiMasi, J. A., R. W. Hansen, H. G. Grabowski, and L. Lasagna. 1991. "Cost of Innovation in the Pharmaceutical Industry." *Journal of Health Economics* 10: 107–42

Eisman, M. M., and W. M. Wardell. 1987. "The Decline in Effective Patent Life of New Drugs." *Research Management* 24: 18–21.

Grabowski, H. G., J. M.Vernon, and L G. Thomas. 1978. "Estimating the Effects of Regulation on Innovation: An International Comparative Analysis of the Pharmaceutical Industry." *Journal of Law and Economics* 21 (1): 133–63.

Hansen, R. W. 1979. "The Pharmaceutical Development Process: Estimates of Development Costs and Times and the Effects of Proposed Regulatory Changes." In *Issues in Pharmaceutical Economics,* ed. R. I. Chien. Lexington, Mass.: Heath.

———. 1981. "Effects of Incremental Costs on Pharmaceutical Innovation." *Economic Costs of FDA Regulations*, ed. Pharmaceutical Manufacturers Association. Washington, D.C.: Pharmaceutical Manufacturers Association.

Kaitin, K. I. 1991. "Case Studies of Expedited Review: AZT and L-Dopa." *Law, Medicine and Health Care* 19(3-4):242-246.

Kaitin, K. I., M. Manocchia, M. Seibring, and L. Lasagna. 1994. "The New Drug Approvals of 1990, 1991, and 1992: Trends in Drug Development." *Journal of Clinical Pharmacology* 34 (2):120–27.

Kaitin, K. I., N. Mattison, F. K. Northington, et al. 1989. "The Drug Lag: An Update of New Drug Introductions in the US and UK., 1977 Through 1987." *Clinical Pharmacology and Therapeutics* 4:121–38.

Lasagna, L. 1989. "Congress, the FDA, and New Drug Development: Before and After 1962." *Perspectives in Biology and Medicine* 32 (3):322–43.

Mattison, N., A. G. Trimble, and L. Lasagna. 1988. "New Drug Development in the United States, 1963 Through 1984." *Clinical Pharmacology and Therapeutics* 43: 290–301.

Merrill, R. A. 1994. "Regulation of Drugs and Devices: An Evolution." *Health Affairs* 13 (3): 47–69.

Salbu, S. R. 1994. "Regulation of Drug Treatments for HIV and AIDS: A Contractarian Model of Access." *Yale Journal of Regulation* 11 (2): 401–53.

U.S. Congress, Office of Technology Assessment. 1993 (February). *Pharmaceutical R&D: Costs, Risks and Rewards*. OTA-H-522. Washington, DC: US. Government Printing Office.

Wardell, W.M. 1973a. "Introduction of New Therapeutic Drugs in the United States and Great Britain: An International Comparison." *Clinical Pharmacology and Therapeutics* 14 (5): 773–90.

———. 1973b. "British Usage and American Awareness of Some New Therapeutic Drugs." *Clinical Pharmacology and Therapeutics* 14 (6): 1022–34.

———. 1978. "The Drug Lag Revisited: Comparisons by Therapeutic Area of Patterns of Drugs Marketed in the US and Great Britain from 1972 Through 1976." *Clinical Pharmacology and Therapeutics* 24: 499–524.

3

FDA Advertising Restrictions: Ignorance Is Death

Paul H. Rubin

Every morning I take an aspirin. The form is a product made by Bayer, "Adult Low Strength Enteric Safety Coated, for Aspirin Regimen Users." The packaging of this product is remarkable. The box indicates that the product is "for the temporary relief of minor aches and pains" but the package insert indicates that "because of its delayed action, BAYER® Enteric Aspirin will not provide fast relief of headaches, fever or other symptoms needing immediate relief." The package insert also suggests that consumers should "Ask your doctor about new uses for BAYER® ENTERIC Aspirin." *But nowhere in any of the materials (the box, the insert, or the bottle itself) is there any indication of the main purpose of this product, or of what these "new uses" might be.*

In fact, this product is made for heart attack prevention. There is substantial medical evidence that taking a daily dose of aspirin can reduce the risk of heart attack in middle-aged males (a category to which I now belong) by almost 50 percent (PHSG 1989). Indeed, the results are so well known that there exists a pamphlet, *Amazing Aspirin* (available for 89¢ at grocery store checkout stands), that discusses this benefit at great length.[1] What is surprising is that neither the package for the aspirin itself nor any advertising for it indicates this valuable use. Why does Bayer forgo the possibility of the increased sales from providing this information to consumers?

On March 2, 1988, at a meeting in the offices of the commissioner of the FDA at the time, Frank Young, all companies making aspirin were

29

told that they could not advertise the benefits of the product in reducing risks for first heart attacks. If they did, the FDA would bring legal action. All of the companies agreed to comply; as of this writing, none of them advertise or promote aspirin for prevention of first heart attacks.[2] The publishers of the 89¢ pamphlet can provide the information because the First Amendment protects them. The FDA does not believe that this Constitutional protection of free speech applies to the pharmaceutical industry.[3]

This episode is important in its own right: the ban on aspirin advertising undoubtedly causes tens of thousands of needless deaths per year. Elimination of this ban would probably be one of the simplest measures available to reduce death rates. In addition to its direct significance, this ban also illustrates several important points about the FDA's general policies with respect to advertising and promotion.[4]

- Much of the FDA's power is extralegal.

- FDA regulation denies consumers and others valuable information.

- The FDA focuses on the risks of advertising and promotion, and neglects the benefits.

- The result of the FDA's policies is that consumers are made less healthy.

I will first discuss these points with respect to aspirin advertising. I will then discuss the two main areas of FDA advertising regulation: advertising of prescription drugs to physicians and direct advertising to consumers. We will see that the policies are extremely harmful, and that the policy with respect to aspirin is indeed typical of the FDA's general behavior.

Aspirin: The Details

I will now consider in detail each of the points made above with respect to the aspirin advertising ban.

Much of the FDA's Power is Extralegal. In the case of aspirin, there was no formal procedure for imposing the ban. At the meeting in the Commissioner's office, the aspirin manufacturers were simply told that they should not advertise aspirin as a first heart attack preventative. The manufacturers complied. Had they not, the FDA would have taken various administrative actions to enforce its policy. Ultimately, if any manufacturer had wanted to pursue the issue far enough, it would have been litigated in court. The firms would then have been able to assert various rights, including the First Amendment right to free speech.

Commercial speech receives less protection from the courts than other forms of speech. Thus, had the matter been litigated, it is possible that the FDA would have succeeded in imposing the ban. It is also possible that the agency would have lost. After all, many authorities believe that the FDA commonly violates the First Amendment to the Constitution when it regulates speech.[5] While the courts have held that false commercial speech does not receive full First Amendment protection, in this case (as in many others involving the FDA) there was no issue of falsity: no one argued that the claims were untrue or that there was any deception. Thus, had the matter gone to the courts, it is at least possible that the FDA would have lost the case.

Why did no firm choose to litigate the issue? Firms are deathly afraid of the FDA, and with good reason. The agency does not merely control advertising of pharmaceutical producers. It controls every aspect of the behavior of such firms. It controls approval of new products. It also inspects firms to make sure they comply with FDA rules regarding manufacturing processes. Thus, firms are generally afraid of antagonizing the FDA, and will commonly agree with regulatory actions rather than litigate. As David Kessler, the current commissioner of the FDA, has put it, "Companies interested in maintaining positive relationships with the FDA usually agree to the FDA's remedy."[6] Thus, the FDA uses its general powers to punish firms to coerce them into actions even when the agency might lack the power to enforce these actions in a legal forum.

FDA Regulation Denies Consumers and Others Valuable Information. This point is quite clear in the case of aspirin. When the reports of the benefits of aspirin were first released, there were stories in newspapers and on TV regarding the findings. Any consumers who happened to read the paper or watch TV on that day would have learned this information. However, a news story itself is a poor way of learning about a procedure that will lead to an actual modification of life style, such as taking a pill every morning. Since then, the fact that aspirin prevents heart attacks is not news, and so is not reported as news. Consumers may read books or magazine articles with this information, such as the pamphlet available at grocery checkout stands. These methods may be useful for some consumers, and particularly for more educated ones. Other consumers can learn about the benefits of aspirin from physicians. However, this is possible only for those who are in regular contact with a physician, and to whom the physician thinks to mention aspirin. Again, these would likely be higher-income consumers. For the mass of consumers who get most of their information from TV and commercials, the FDA's ban essentially means that they do not learn that their lives could be lengthened by taking aspirin.[7] Moreover, a news story cannot report on new forms and dosages of aspirin, such as the low dose pill I take daily.

> ***The FDA Focuses on the Risks of Advertising and Promotion, and Neglects the Benefits.*** Why does the FDA have this policy with respect to aspirin advertising? One semi-official statement is from David Adams, associate chief counsel for drugs for the FDA.

> In another interesting case, a group of aspirin makers suggested the possibility of press conferences to present to the public new evidence on the beneficial effects of a daily aspirin regimen in preventing heart attacks in individuals who had not previously had a heart attack. Although this information was important, the agency was concerned that, for some individuals, the risk of having a heart attack might be less than the risk of other, harmful effects posed by the aspirin regimen. The agency impressed on the drug companies that this sort of education should come from physicians rather than from a press conference by an aspirin manufacturer. (Adams 1992, 56–57)

The "harmful effects" refer to a slightly increased risk of a certain type of stroke for some individuals if aspirin is used. However, the level of increase in this risk is small; indeed, it is not even statistically significant. The reduction in risk of heart attack from taking aspirin for the middle-aged males tremendously outweighs the slightly increased risk of stroke. Moreover, advertising and promotion could easily indicate that aspirin is not a suitable drug for young females and any other group for whom the risks might outweigh the benefits.

This behavior is typical of the FDA. It invariably places a much greater weight on any potential harm from a pharmaceutical than on any benefit from the product. This explains the tremendous delays in FDA approval of new drugs: the agency is much more fearful of approving a harmful drug than of delaying or blocking a beneficial drug. The FDA's timidity in allowing advertising and promotion of drugs is based on the same fear. The result is excess deaths.[8]

It is also true that the FDA has not approved aspirin for heart attack prevention. Part of the reason is that no manufacturer has applied for such approval. The FDA's approval process is costly, and it would cost some tens or hundreds of millions of dollars to obtain approval for aspirin as a heart attack preventative.[9] Indeed, because the benefits of aspirin are so well documented, it might be impossible for ethical reasons to undertake such a study at all; researchers would probably be unwilling to deny any patients the benefits of aspirin, as is required in such a study. The one study cited previously (PHSG 1989) was terminated early because of the overwhelming evidence of the benefits of aspirin. But even if the study were possible, no manufacturer would be willing to finance it. This is because aspirin is no longer covered by a patent, so any manufacturer could use the results of a study in selling its product. In other words, any firm undertaking this research would be unable to reap the benefits. This is often the case for drugs available in generic versions as well. However, the case is worse for aspirin: not only is the product not covered by a patent, but the name ("Aspirin") has lost its trademark protection.

The Result of the FDA's Policies Is that Consumers Are Made Less Healthy. By now, this point should be obvious. It is possible that a small number of consumers have benefited from the FDA's policies because they might have inappropriately taken aspirin and suffered strokes. However, many more consumers have been harmed than have benefited. In particular, middle-aged males (and many females) who would have learned of the benefits of aspirin from a vigorous advertising campaign have been denied this benefit. Indeed, Bayer tried to market enteric-coated aspirin (the sort most useful for heart attack prevention) in a "blister" pack, designed for daily use, but the FDA forbade even this form of marketing.

Advertising of Prescription Drugs to Physicians

FDA regulation of advertising and promotion of prescription drugs can best be understood if we consider promotion to physicians and to consumers separately. In this section, I will consider advertising to physicians; in the next section, I consider consumers.

Benefits of Promotion. One sometimes sees criticisms of the amount the pharmaceutical industry spends on promotion. A typical complaint will be that the industry spends as much or more on promotion as on research and development (for example, see Chren 1992). Such complaints are fundamentally misguided and demonstrate a lack of understanding of the industry and of the purpose of promotional expenditures.

In one sense, promotional expenditures are not different from expenditures on research. Begin with some chemical of unknown properties. Then research is a way of determining what these properties are and what, if any, uses the chemical has as a drug; that is, research expenditures are a way of obtaining information about the drug. The culmination of this spending is the approval by the FDA of the drug for marketing.

But at this point the drug has no economic value. Moreover, no matter how useful the drug may be, it has little value as a medicine. This is because the information in the research already conducted is valueless until physicians who will prescribe the drug are aware of the information. The way physicians obtain this information is through advertising and promotion. Without this spending, the drug will not be prescribed and will not be available to cure patients. Research and advertising are both information-generating activities.

A recent study found that promotional spending by pharmaceutical companies increased the sales of their products (Chren and Landefeld 1994). Physicians were more likely to request addition of products to hospital formularies (lists of acceptable drugs for use in the hospital) if they had been involved with the promotional activities of the pharmaceutical company. This result is, of course, not surprising. After all, the purpose of promotion is to promote. However, the interpretation of these results is important. Some might interpret the findings as indicating that pharmaceutical companies unduly influence behavior of physicians through promotional expenditures. At least one of the authors, Chren, has been a critic of pharmaceutical promotional expenditures, as mentioned previously. However, this interpretation should be resisted.

Rather, the article documents the social benefits of information provision by pharmaceutical companies; it indicates that all of the 55 requests for addition of new drugs to the formulary were at the request of physicians, often after interactions with drug companies. Thirteen of the requests were for drugs that represented a major therapeutic advance over existing drugs, and 13 for drugs with a modest therapeutic advantage. Thus, the study indicates that pharmaceutical promotion was responsible for the addition of these drugs to the hospital formulary. Without such promotion, it is less likely that the drugs would have been made available to patients.

There were recommendations to add 29 drugs to the formulary that had no clinical advantages over existing drugs; 23 of these drugs were approved for addition. Price information regarding the drugs is not given in the article. It is likely that some of the 29 drugs that were reported as having little or no therapeutic advantage were lower priced than existing drugs; this is particularly likely for the 23 of these drugs that were actually added to the formulary. Competition from drugs with similar clinical profiles is the most powerful force restraining drug prices. Thus, this study indicates some of the benefits of promotional expenditures.

There is additional evidence of the value of pharmaceutical promotion. A recent study examined behavior of "expert" physicians, those writing medical textbooks and review articles in medical journals (Antman et al. 1992). This study found that experts writing about myocardial infarction (heart attacks) in many cases recommended treatments that were "several years" behind the best data available. Thus, the evidence indicates that physicians do not receive enough information about new drugs. If more resources were spent on promotion, patient health would improve.

There are some additional examples of the benefits of promotion.[10] First, the National Cholesterol Education Program increased the awareness of the danger of high cholesterol among physicians from 39 to 64 percent within two years. The number of adults who had had their cholesterol checked increased from 35 percent in 1983 to 66 percent in 1989. Second, a campaign for its hepatitis B vaccine by Smith Kline Beacham publicizing the OSHA guidelines requiring employers to offer certain employees free vaccines against this disease was associated with a significant decline in the incidence of hepatitis B.

Regulation of Promotion. One reason why more is not spent on promotion is the excessive regulation of promotion and advertising by the FDA. The FDA has always taken a very expansive view of its authority to regulate advertising and promotion. As the commissioner of the FDA indicates,

> The [Food, Drug and Cosmetic] Act does not define what constitutes an advertisement, but the FDA generally views anything, other than labeling, that promotes a drug product and that is sponsored by a manufacturer as advertising…The definitions of labeling and advertising taken together cover —at least in the FDA's opinion — virtually all information disseminating activities by or on behalf of a prescription drug manufacturer.[11]

While regulation of pharmaceutical advertising has always been excessive, in recent years this regulation has greatly increased and become more harmful. In order to fully understand this increase in regulation, we must first define the concepts of "approved" and "unapproved" uses of a drug. When a pharmaceutical firm obtains approval for a drug, the drug is approved only for certain uses; these are the uses in the application filed with the FDA and on the drug label. (Approved uses are also called "on-label" uses.) Other potential uses of the drug are "unapproved" (or "off-label") uses. For example, in the previous discussion of aspirin, the use of aspirin as a first heart attack preventative would be an off-label use.

There is nothing wrong with using a drug for an unapproved, or off-label, use. Physicians are free to prescribe drugs for any purposes they feel are desirable. Often, as in the case of aspirin, there will be substantial medical evidence published in journals attesting to the efficacy of a drug for an off-label use. One third of drugs given to cancer patients are for unapproved uses, and an estimated one-fourth of all U.S. prescriptions are for such uses (Beales 1994, 1386). Of particular importance are drugs for pediatric cancer, since the low incidence of cancer in children means that manufacturers will seldom seek approval for such uses. Instead, physicians will commonly use drugs approved for adults in treating children. Off-label uses for drugs may also be listed in various medical compendia (lists of uses of drugs).[12]

There are various reasons why a use may be off-label. A firm may be in the process of obtaining FDA approval for the new use. It can take a long time for such approval to be granted. Requests for "supplementary" approval are often given lower priority by the FDA than initial requests. One study has found that requests for original approval take an average of 23.5 months, that requests for supplemental uses take an average of 21.5 months, and that these delays are not significantly different.[13] Moreover, a firm may never obtain such approval. As mentioned in the case of aspirin, if a patent has expired, then it will not pay for a firm to spend the required money to obtain such approval. Even if the patent has not yet expired, as a drug gets older, the length of time until the patent will expire becomes shorter. Thus, it may not pay for a firm to spend the money to obtain supplementary approval when the time to benefit from this approval will be shorter than for the initial use.

The FDA forbids advertising of off-label uses. Since these uses are important, this policy is harmful. There is evidence, for example, that sales of drugs for newly approved uses increase dramatically after approval, because of promotion, even though the drug was available for this use before approval (Beales 1994, 1391). And in recent years, the FDA has increased regulation of nonadvertising efforts of pharmaceutical companies to inform physicians of unapproved uses. For example, it is now often illegal for pharmaceutical companies to send reprints of scientific articles reporting research on this class of use to physicians. A drug company can send reprints if "there is an unsolicited request for the information. If the detail man has suggested to the physician that he request such information from the company, the agency [FDA] will regard the activity as promotional" (Adams 1992, 63). It is also difficult for these companies to sponsor symposia and seminars for physicians to inform them of such uses. Moreover, for FDA regulation, truth of a claim is not a defense: "Such promotion is prohibited even if these uses are supported by studies in the medical literature" (Kessler and Pines 1990, 2411).

Thus, the agency since about 1991 has increased regulation and virtually prohibited promotion of off-label uses. Moreover, this change in policy was on the basis of a "Draft Concept Paper" that the FDA never officially adopted; this is another example of use of extralegal authority by the agency (discussed in Levine 1993). This policy means that it will take longer for the medical community to learn about some uses of drugs and, since firms never seek approval for some uses, it will be impossible for manufacturers to ever promote many uses of drugs. This policy has been extremely harmful (see Calfee 1992).

As suggested above, pharmaceutical companies have been unwilling to challenge this policy. The Washington Legal Foundation (WLF), a public interest law firm in Washington, D.C., has protested the FDA policy. The foundation first filed a Citizen Petition. Interestingly, although eight groups (one of which is an umbrella for nine additional organizations) filed comments in support of the WLF, none of these groups represented pharmaceutical manufacturers. More recently, the WLF has filed a suit against the FDA regarding promotion of off-label uses.

Benefits of Regulation: Are Ads Deceptive?[14] The benefits of regulation and restriction of pharmaceutical advertising may be measured in terms of reduction of deception. This raises the issue of the amount of deception in pharmaceutical ads. For several reasons, we would not expect much deception. Pharmaceutical companies are major firms, and reputations of large firms are valuable assets, so firms avoid deception whenever possible (discussed, for example, in Rubin 1990). This would be even more true for pharmaceutical firms than for others, since customers of pharmaceutical firms, physicians, are skilled buyers and also repeat customers. If such customers learn that a company was deceptive with respect to one product, they are more likely than most customers to discount all advertising by that company. There is also evidence that firms engaging in deception lose substantial amounts of value when deception in advertising is detected (Peltzman 1981; Mathios and Plummer 1989). Thus, we would not expect much deception in pharmaceutical advertising.

Contrary to these expectations, some claim that there is evidence of such deception. A recent article in the *Annals of Internal Medicine* examined advertisements for pharmaceuticals in medical journals (Wilkes, Doblin, and Shapiro 1992). The popular press reported the results of this study widely, and interpreted it as finding that ads were "often misleading" (New York Times, June 1, 1992, p. 1). Partially as a result of this study, there are proposals to require preapproval of ads by an independent review group or by the FDA. There is a proposed bill, H.R. 5485, introduced by California Congressman Pete Stark, that would deny tax deductibility to prescription drug advertisements not approved by an independent review board. If adopted, this policy would lead to examination of all ads by such a board. It is unfortunate that the *Annals* report is proving so influential, because there are serious problems with the analysis.

The study was a survey of physicians and pharmacists regarding their views of a sample of pharmaceutical advertisements. All ads of at least one page from the first issue of 1990 from 10 medical journals were in the sample. After elimination of duplicates, there were 109 such ads. Each ad was sent to three reviewers, two physicians with experience in the area of medicine relevant to the ad and an academic clinical pharmacist. Reviewers were asked a total of 36 questions about each ad. Of these, 28 questions were based on FDA regulations and eight were more general questions. Ads were evaluated with respect to a particular issue only if two or more of the reviewers felt that the issue was relevant. For example, in 53 of the 109 cases, two or more reviewers believed that the drug was promoted as "the drug of choice" for some condition. Questions regarding the appropriateness of that claim were evaluated only for those 53 drugs.

The key findings of the analysis were as follows: Reviewers concluded that 92 percent of the ads were not in full compliance with FDA criteria in one or more of the 28 categories examined. With respect to educational value: 20 percent of the ads were judged to have none; 37 percent to have little; 33 percent to have some; and 4 percent to have a great deal. With respect to prescribing behavior, "Only 44 percent of reviewers felt that the advertisement would lead to proper prescribing if a physician had no other information about the medicine other than that presented in the advertisement. There was no agreement [between the reviewers] for 6 percent of the advertisements."

The final question was, "If this advertisement were subject to the same review criteria as a scientific article, would your overall suggestion to a journal editor be to accept in present form, accept contingent on minor revisions, accept contingent on major revisions, or reject the advertisement?" In 76 cases, there was agreement by two or more reviewers on appropriateness of publication. On this basis, 28 percent of the ads would have been rejected, 34 percent would have required major revision, 35 percent minor revision, and 4 percent would have been accepted without change.

Thus, as reported, the results of the study imply that there are serious problems with pharmaceutical advertising. However, flaws in the study mean that these results have little if any relevance to policy.

First, note that at no time did the authors of the study attempt to determine if the respondents themselves were deceived, or if anyone else was actually misled. Rather, the import of the questions was to ask if the respondents *believed* that others would be deceived by the ads. But the respondents were not experts in deception or in psychology. Thus, the fundamental research paradigm on which the article was based was misspecified. For example, as a professional economist, I may be able to evaluate the economic content of newspaper articles reporting on economics, but I cannot evaluate the impact of these articles on readers of newspapers. Such evaluation requires market research techniques that were not included in the study. I do not use such techniques here, but they provide an alternative method of evaluating the study.[15]

The analysis that follows is based on the article itself. In performing this analysis, I did not have access to the actual data generated by the authors. An analysis that did have access to the data also finds flaws in the study; for example, it concludes that "Because of numerous methodological flaws in constructing the survey instrument and conducting the study, no conclusion can be drawn that the advertisements reviewed misled physicians....What little can be gleaned from the article suggests that advertising is performing its function of delivering information, which in the vast majority of cases is unlikely to mislead physicians" (Beales and MacLeod 1995).

I analyze the study from the perspective of the economics of information. This approach begins with the observation that information is both valuable and costly. Thus, an economist asks about incentives of relevant parties to provide and absorb information. While this approach recognizes that deception is possible, the method of analysis also pays particular attention to the information that would be lost if the ads were eliminated or restricted. The approach also pays attention to consumers of information. Time of consumers of advertising (whether direct consumers or their agents, such as physicians) is also expensive, and information must be provided in a manner that will reduce costs of absorbing the information. Producers of goods are often in the best position to provide such information in a way that will be effective. Consumers also come to the market with information of their own, so an important issue is the interaction of new information with the information already in existence.

To students of the FDA, this approach may seem novel. This is because the FDA regulates promotion and advertising from a perspective that does not generally include these considerations. However, the Federal Trade Commission (FTC), the major body charged with regulating advertising, does consider exactly these questions in its decisions regarding regulation of advertising.[16]

The authors of the *Annals* study, who are academic physicians, claim to find that ads are misleading and that greater regulation of advertising is needed. Their basic point is that ads do not meet proper standards. I consider each of the major points in the article. These points are (1) the extent to which the ads meet FDA standards, (2) the amount of educational value in the ads, (3) the effect of ads on prescribing behavior, (4) the extent to which the ads would meet the criteria required for articles to be accepted for publication in a refereed journal, and (5) the article's policy suggestions.

FDA Standards. A key point was that the reviewers believed that many ads violated at least one FDA standard.[17] The reviewers were not trained in the use of FDA standards by FDA officials, and did not necessarily evaluate the ads as would these officials. Many of the rules require judgment: they are full of terms such as "appropriate," "likely to mislead," and "adequate." These terms do not have objective meanings; they are regulatory terms of art, and can be defined only in the context of normal enforcement strategies. Some authorities believe that almost any ad could be found "deceptive" under some readings (Craswell 1985).

This is not meant as a critique of the FDA. Any legal standard will require elaboration, either through administrative clarification or through a common law process. The point is simply that the unguided intuition of a physician or pharmacist is not likely to derive the most useful meaning of such legalistic terms. The FTC, which also regulates "deception," has spent thousands of internal staff hours debating the meaning of such terms, and no doubt the FDA has as well.

Moreover, FDA bureaucrats, like all law enforcement officials, use "prosecutorial discretion" in deciding which matters are worth attention. The FDA regulations are so broad that it is almost impossible to write an ad that does not technically violate some rule, which may be why the study purports to find that 92 percent of the ads did violate FDA standards. But FDA officials wisely ignore many purely technical violations, even in a climate where enforcement efforts have greatly increased in recent years. The reviewers of ads in this study did not, and so were likely to focus on trivial "violations" of FDA rules.

Finally, in evaluating compliance with FDA standards, it is important to note that the ads contained the FDA-mandated brief summary (described in the following section on direct advertising to consumers). A plausible scenario for a physician reading an ad is to first read the ad itself. If the medicine appears promising, the physician might then turn to the brief summary for further data. Under this scenario, most physicians would ignore the brief summary because they would have no interest in the product, but those actually considering prescribing the medicine would read it.

Educational Value. The authors also report that the reviewers believed the ads had relatively little educational value. The authors do not provide a definition of "educational value." If they define educational value in the sense of the information provided in a lecture or in a journal article, then the measure is meaningless. For example, many ads are reminder ads, which do not purport to have any educational value. These ads are aimed at keeping the name of the drug before the physician who already prescribes the drug. Other ads indicate that an existing medicine is available in a new dosage or new form. To criticize these ads for lacking educational value is inappropriate.

A more useful question would be to ask if the ads provide *any* information. Here, the answer would of necessity be different. In one sense, any ad provides information. First, the ad indicates that the manufacturer has enough confidence in the product to spend resources advertising it; this alone is valuable information to prospective purchasers. Of course, this information is not definitive, but it is nonetheless valuable. If advertisers believed that a physician would prescribe a product only once or a few times and then cease using it, they would not find the product worth advertising.[18] Second, even if the ad mentions only a drug and a condition, the physician is alerted that this product may be worth further examination. Indeed, this appears to be the major message conveyed by almost all pharmaceutical ads.[19]

Prescribing Behavior. The study also claims that many of the ads would lead to improper prescribing behavior *if the physician had no information other than that found in the ad.* It is impossible to evaluate the ability of ads to deceive in a vacuum. Readers always have some prior information. By making alternative assumptions about the amount of this information, it is possible to find that any ad is deceptive. This is why marketing research techniques (which measure the effects of ads on actual consumers with actual prior sets of information) are necessary to truly measure deception.

The hypothesis that the physician has no other information is clearly incorrect. Physicians have 10 or more years of training and access to journal articles, medical texts, and other sources of information. If the authors wanted information about this point, a more reasonable question would have asked if the ad would lead to improper prescribing behavior *if the physician had the amount of information we would expect a normal, practicing physician to possess.* Even then, the authors would rely on one set of physicians and pharmacists to guess what another set of physicians will learn from some ads. They provide no evidence that any ad actually deceived anyone. Indeed, the methodology of their study made it impossible to determine if there was actual deception.

Moreover, consider the ads themselves. For an ad to lead to improper prescribing behavior means that there is some more appropriate drug that doctors should prescribe. If so, physicians would also have access to ads for this more appropriate remedy, and to assume that the physician has no other information ignores information that was itself part of the study. While these additional ads might not provide all the information a physician needs to properly prescribe, it is nonetheless improper to ignore them totally, as does the phrasing of the question ("no other information").

The set of ads examined in the study apparently does provide exactly this sort of information. The reviewers found 66 ads (for 62 drugs) to deserve rejection or major revision. Of these ads, only 11 were for drugs from a class with less than four competing drugs in the sample itself. For antibiotics, there were 24 competing ads in the sample (of which the report criticized 17). While not all of these drugs would compete with each other, there are probably few, if any, conditions for which only one drug would be advertised. In other words, in most cases, drugs competed against other advertised drugs in the sample itself. Undoubtedly, many other drugs that did not advertise in the sample month or in the sample journals compete and provide information useful to physicians for comparing those drugs that did advertise in the sample.

Many of the ads themselves provide names of competing products, so that a physician would know exactly which products to consider in comparing the advertised product with alternatives. Thus, it is improper to argue that the ads exist in a vacuum. Just as aspirin, ibuprofen, and acetaminophen ads provide competing information to consumers of over-the-counter headache remedies, so prescription drugs advertising to physicians provide competing information. To claim that ads would lead to improper prescribing behavior if the physician had no other information is contradicted by the ads themselves, which provide other information.

In a response to various critics, Wilkes, Doblin, and Shapiro (1992b) claim that "advertisements profoundly influence the way prescription drugs are used in our society...all too often, they are the decisive source of information about new pharmaceutical products." But this skirts the issue: an ad may be influential in leading to prescribing behavior if the ad only directs attention to a new product and if the physician then seeks additional information about the product. By implying in their response that ads do more than this, the authors are themselves being somewhat deceptive.

Peer Review. Recall that the last question asked reviewers was, "If this advertisement were subject to the same review criteria as a scientific article, would your overall suggestion to a journal editor be to accept in present form, accept contingent on minor revisions, accept contingent on major revisions, or reject the advertisement?" Many of the reviewers would have rejected the ads or required major revisions. However, this information is not useful.

It is inappropriate to expect ads to meet the same standards as refereed journal articles, or to evaluate ads using the criteria relevant for such articles. Nothing meets these standards except these articles. For example, no newspaper article (including those reporting the results of the study) would meet these standards. But this misses the point. Readers know what they are reading. A physician knows that an ad does not serve the same purpose as a refereed article and does not meet the same standards. Readers of newspapers, for example, do not place the same faith in the ads as in the text. Many of the ads contain only a few lines of text.

Obviously, such an ad would not meet standards for publication as an article; just as obviously, no reader would expect the ad to meet these standards.

If we sent 100 medical journal articles to advertising directors, they would find all 100 poorly written and incoherent. This could lead to the headline "Study finds medical research uninformative and ill-presented." The result from such a study would tell us nothing about articles in medical journals because the study would be based on use of inappropriate criteria.

Peer review is not itself legally required for any purpose. Medical and other academic journals have decided that this method of screening articles is worthwhile because it increases the credibility of the articles and therefore the value of the journal to readers. If medical editors felt that peer review of ads would make their journals more valuable, or if drug manufacturers felt this, then either party could voluntarily engage in such review and publicize this practice. There is no need for an outside party to mandate such scrutiny, just as no one has mandated this process for current journals.

Policy Suggestions. For a criticism to be helpful, it must contain suggestions for improvement. This is where the study shows its greatest weaknesses. The authors suggest, "One approach would be to ban pharmaceutical advertising from journals." This would be useful only if the net effect of the existing ads were to reduce the information available to physicians, a claim that the study never makes or even considers. The authors reject this proposal only because they claim that other methods of promotion are even more difficult to regulate, not because they understand that the effect would be to reduce available information. The authors of the study are primarily academics, not practicing physicians, and one gets the feeling that they believe physicians should obtain all information from articles in medical journals. This would greatly reduce the time available for practice and increase the costs of medical care, but the authors are apparently indifferent to costs borne by consumers.

Another suggestion is for increased FDA enforcement of existing regulations. The authors realize that any program would impose additional costs, but they believe that the costs should be "borne by the manufacturers." Economic analysis clearly indicates that any increased cost will result in higher prices paid by consumers.

Based on this article, some have suggested that an independent review board be created to review all pharmaceutical ads. A requirement for preapproval of advertisements for pharmaceuticals would lead to delays in drug advertising, to fewer ads, and to reduced information in each ad. There is no doubt that such a review process would greatly reduce the number of advertisements. It also would increase the cost of advertising and would mean that ads would take longer to reach their audience. During the delay, physicians would be denied valuable information, particularly about new products or new uses of existing products.

Moreover, it is likely that ads approved by a board would provide less information than ads written by the companies, because such a board would be innately conservative. Consider the problems faced by a company in drafting an ad. The company wants to make expansive claims in order to increase sales. However, there are risks from claims that are too expansive. If a claim is made with insufficient support, there may be regulatory penalties. In addition, physicians who learn that a particular company makes unreliable claims for its products will discount future claims for all products made by this company. Thus, the company has incentives to try to sell the product but to avoid any costs of making insufficiently based claims.

A review board is subject to only one side of this equation. The board would have an incentive to disallow any claim that is at all doubtful because the board gains nothing from additional sales but will be subject to criticism if any claim turns out to be unreliable. Thus, there would be incentives for the board to be excessively cautious in approving claims. The result would likely be reduced information to physicians about useful drugs and thus reduced health of consumers. Indeed, the results of the Wilkes et al. study itself demonstrate this. Here, a group of outside "experts" found almost all ads subject to criticism, even though all pharmaceutical companies have intense internal reviews of ads (discussed in Cooper 1992). If there were an external review of ads, we would expect that most of them would need to be rewritten at least once, adding to delay and denying physicians information in the ads.

Thus, we may conclude that there is no evidence that pharmaceutical ads are deceptive. Since the benefits of regulation would be in terms of reduced deception, there is no evidence of a need for increased regulation. Moreover, since we saw earlier that physicians have too little information, an attempt to increase regulation of pharmaceutical ads would clearly be misguided.

Direct Advertising to Consumers [20]

Benefits of Direct Advertising
Health Benefits. Analysis of direct-to-consumer advertising has identified several health benefits. These benefits accrue because consumers have information about themselves that is not readily accessible to a physician. The information known only to individual consumers about their own health status can sometimes be combined with information in pharmaceutical ads to better match patients and drugs. We identify the following benefits from direct advertising:

1. A consumer may not be aware that a treatment exists for some condition, and so will not consult a physician. Two prominent examples are Upjohn's Rogaine®, a treatment for some conditions of baldness, and Marion Merrell Dow's Nicorette® gum. In both cases, consumers may not be aware that there exist prescription remedies for the conditions unless informed by advertising. More recently, Rogaine® has been aiming its ads at women suffering from hair loss. Nicorette® is particularly interesting because cigarette manufacturers can advertise with only a brief, one-line mention of health risks, but a remedy is required to have a lengthy "brief summary." Moreover, most of this brief summary discusses the dangers of nicotine, but if consumers were not aware of these dangers they would not want to quit smoking anyway.

2. A consumer may suffer some symptoms (e.g., thirst) without realizing that these are symptoms of a disease (e.g., diabetes). A consumer who does not realize that symptoms indicate a disease will not consult a physician and therefore cannot learn in this way that he has a treatable disease. For example, recent ads for Merck's Proscar® indicate that urinary problems may be symptomatic of prostate enlargement, and that there is a non-surgical treatment for this condition.

3. A consumer may have been previously diagnosed with some then untreatable disease for which a new treatment has since become available. Because the consumer believes that the disease is not treatable, or because previous remedies have been ineffective, she may not contact a physician and therefore may not learn about the new therapy. Advertisements can inform her and lead to treatment. A similar analysis applies to the creation of a new vaccine or preventative for a condition to which some consumers may know themselves to be susceptible. An example is a vaccine for hepatitis B, a disease to which homosexuals are particularly susceptible. Ads for Wyeth-Ayerst's Premarin® and Ciba-Geigy's Estraderm® indicate that these post-menopausal medicines can reduce the chance for osteoporosis, and some of the ads provide information about susceptibility to this condition.

4. A new remedy with reduced side effects may become available. Advertising can provide benefits in two cases. Consumers who do not know that symptoms they are experiencing are side effects, and so would not ask a physician about them, may learn from ads that there are alternatives without these side effects. Consumers who have ceased treatment because of side effects, and so are not seeing a physician, may begin treatment again if they learn of therapies that do not impose the same side effects.

An example is impotence caused by some antihypertensives. Some consumers may not know that the condition is drug related; others may have stopped therapy because of the condition. Either class of consumers can benefit from ads indicating that a treatment with reduced side effects is available. Other examples include the Marion Merrell Dow campaign for Seldane-D® and the Janssen Pharmaceutica campaign for Hismanal® as allergy medicines less likely to cause drowsiness.

5. A medication may simply be available that is more convenient than existing medications. For example, Searle advertises Daypro® as an arthritis medicine that can be taken only once a day, and Depo-Provera® is advertised as a method of birth control that does not require daily medication. A physician might not be aware that the less convenient form is a problem for a particular consumer. Alternatively, a consumer might have stopped using the medication because of the inconvenience, and so might not be in contact with a physician. Thus, direct advertising in this instance can be quite useful.

For all of these cases, it is important to remember that a physician must approve the purchase of all of the medicines under consideration. Thus, if an ad misleads a consumer, there is an immediate check. The only cost to the consumer is the cost of a (perhaps) superfluous visit to a physician. On the other hand, the cost of not allowing the advertising is that some consumers may needlessly suffer the symptoms of disease, when treatments are available. This health cost will generally outweigh the money cost of the visit to the physician.

Price Reductions. Direct-to-consumer advertising will also lead to price reductions for pharmaceuticals. There is evidence from many markets that increased advertising leads to lower prices.[21] The Supreme Court cited this evidence in decisions overturning state bans on advertising of attorney services and of eyeglasses. Price is currently less effective as a competitive tool in pharmaceuticals than in many other lines of commerce because the physician chooses the product but the consumer has to pay for it. Therefore, providing information to consumers enabling them to compare prices more easily would have a larger than average effect on price because this advertising would provide information to the party actually paying for the product.

There are several mechanisms through which advertising can lead to lower prices. Advertising can inform consumers that two versions of the same drug (a branded version and a generic) are effectively equivalent. Consumers can also learn that two different drugs are effectively equivalent and that one is cheaper, and thus ask physicians to prescribe the lower-priced product. For example, an ad campaign for Ciba-Geigy's Lotensin® indicates that it is cheaper than Capoten® or Vasotec®, competing blood pressure medicines. Increased competition brought about by increased advertising can lead manufacturers to reduce prices for drugs. If one ad can simultaneously list the use of a drug, the price, and the name, then price competition between retail pharmacies can be increased.[22] As of today, an ad cannot provide all of this information without including the "brief summary."

Current Regulations: the "Brief Summary". It is impossible to understand regulation of drug advertising to consumers without understanding the "brief summary of prescribing information." This document is a distillation of the package insert, required in all pharmaceuticals. It is a technical summary of the uses, side effects and contraindications of a drug. (A contraindication is a condition making the use of a particular drug undesirable. For example, for some drugs pregnancy may be a contraindication. Some drugs should not be taken together, so use of one drug may be a contraindication for another drug.) This brief summary (brief only in bureaucratic terms) must be included with (almost) all advertising of the drug. It is a technical document, written for physicians and other professionals, and virtually incomprehensible to consumers. It is the small, difficult-to-read type that always follows an ad for a drug.

The regulations regarding the document are bizarre and could have been produced only by a bureaucracy. They can best be understood by defining those ads that do not require a brief summary. If an ad mentions only the name of a drug but not its use or purpose, then the brief summary is not required. (For example, an ad saying that "Rogaine® is now on sale" without mentioning hair loss would not require a brief summary.) Similarly, if an ad mentions that some treatment is available from a physician for some condition but does not mention that the treatment is a drug, then a brief summary is not needed. An example is Glaxo's discussion of heartburn, ultimately aimed at selling Zantac®, which, however, is not mentioned in the ad. If the ad mentions a drug and a condition, then a brief summary is required, even if the ad does not mention the name of the drug or the producer.

Although the rules make only bureaucratic sense, the FDA enforces them with nit-picking zeal. In one case, an advertiser was required to change the wording of a message in an ad from "Now there's an effective treatment your doctor can prescribe" to "Your doctor can prescribe an effective treatment program" (cited in Kessler and Pines, 1990, 2413). In another case, an actor was prohibited from scratching his head during a Rogaine® commercial because the FDA believed that this indicated that the product was related to hair.

Although these policies seem ludicrous, they in fact have substantial detrimental effects. The requirement of a brief summary adds greatly to the cost of print ads. The brief summary will often be as long as or longer than the ad itself; thus, on average, this requirement probably doubles the cost of print advertising, and therefore reduces the quantity. More important, the requirement for a brief summary makes it virtually impossible to advertise prescription medicines on TV; indeed, this may be one purpose of the requirement (Kessler and Pines 1990, 2413). This reduces greatly the amount of information available to consumers. Moreover, it is less-educated consumers who are most likely to get information from TV, and so who are most likely to be harmed by this policy.

Summary

When we think of the FDA and overregulation, we tend to think of the inexcusable delays in approval of new drugs. Scholars have long been aware that the agency causes unnecessary deaths and suffering by this policy. Nothing in this chapter is to be interpreted as minimizing this cause of needless suffering.

But this is only part of the problem with the FDA. Once the FDA approves a drug, users must learn of it. This can occur through advertising and promotion either to physicians or directly to consumers. In both cases, the FDA's policies greatly retard the spread of such information. This set of policies also has substantial detrimental effects on health. Moreover, in recent years, the FDA has become more regulatory, even as evidence of the harm of its behavior mounts. One policy, the banning of advertising of aspirin for first heart attack prevention, may be the single most harmful regulatory policy currently pursued by any agency of the U.S. government.

What policies might correct this problem? One suggestion is to give regulatory power over pharmaceutical advertising and promotion to another agency, such as the Federal Trade Commission (FTC).[23] The FTC had this jurisdiction until 1962, so the reform would not be a radical departure. This shift in power would be appropriate not because the FTC is a more enlightened agency, but because it has less power over pharmaceutical companies and therefore could not regulate in as arbitrary and capricious a manner as does the FDA. If it tried to enforce counterproductive regulations, companies would be more likely to challenge it in court, and would sometimes win.

If reform does not go this far, several intermediate steps are available. The FDA should immediately cancel all its recent initiatives reducing promotion of off-label uses and return to the pre-Kessler world. The FDA should allow manufacturers to advertise any claim for which reliable scientific evidence exists, whether or not this claim has been approved for the label, and this advertising should be allowed for both consumers and physicians. No policy requiring prior approval of advertisements should be mandated, by Congress or by the FDA. With respect to ads to consumers, the requirement of the "brief summary" should be abolished. The FDA should allow free and unrestricted advertising of pharmaceuticals on TV and in print, subject only to regulation for "falsity" but not for "deception" as currently defined. The results will be greatly improved health of consumers and reduced prices of pharmaceuticals.

Notes

1. This publication is by no means a scientific gem. For example, it has an ad for horoscopes on the inside front cover. Nonetheless, the consumer information about aspirin seems accurate.

2. This meeting is described in detail in Mann and Plummer 1991. Aspirin can be advertised as a preventative for a second heart attack, and some Bayer advertising does make this point.

3. Discussed at length in Kaplar 1993.

4. The regulation of aspirin advertising is atypical in one sense. Generally, the FDA regulates advertising of prescription drugs, and the Federal Trade Commission (FTC) regulates advertising of over-the-counter (OTC) drugs. Regulation of an OTC drug by the FDA is thus anomalous. However, other aspects of this regulation are typical.

5. See the discussion in Kaplar 1993.

6. Kessler and Pines 1990, 2410. This article was written before Kessler became commissioner of the FDA, but it appears to express his views as commissioner as well.

7. This point has been documented in detail for fiber in diets. When cereal makers began advertising that fiber was healthy, the main beneficiaries were relatively less-educated, lower-income consumers. See Ippolito and Mathios 1990.

8. The original research showing excessive delays was by Sam Peltzman (1973). A summary of the literature appears in Comanor 1986. Recent discussions are available in Kazman 1990 and Ward 1992. A legal analysis is in Breckner 1993.

9. On average, it costs $359 million to develop a new drug (PMA 1993, 91). Since most of this cost is for clinical testing, the costs of seeking approval for a new use for aspirin would be in this range.

10. These are from PRMA 1994, sec. 12, which also contains additional examples.

11. Kessler and Pines 1990, 2410, footnotes omitted.

12. The major compendia are American Hospital Formulary Drug Service Information; American Medical Association Drug Evaluations; and U.S. Pharmacopoeia Drug Information.

13. Cited in PMA 1993, at 23.2.

14. This section is based on Rubin 1994. That paper has a more detailed analysis and provides some additional criticisms of the article. Some of the arguments made here were briefly raised in Rubin 1992, p. A8.

15. These points are elaborated on in Jacoby 1994, which does apply marketing research techniques to the study.

16. I was director of the Division of Consumer Protection in the Bureau of Economics at the FTC from 1983 to 1985, and my research on the advertising policies of the FDA began at that time; see Masson and

Rubin 1985. Some published materials detailing the economic approach are Beales, Craswell, and Salop 1981, Craswell 1985, Calfee 1994, and Rubin 1991a. All of these authors spent time at the FTC. The last study has an extensive bibliography on the economics of information and deception, and applies the analysis to many FDA policies.

17. While some of these standards were important, others are more doubtful. For example, 31 ads were faulted for "headlines or subheadlines" that were not "adequately referenced" (table 3).

18. This is a standard economic point in analyzing advertising. It was first made by Philip Nelson (1974). Applications to deception are in Rubin 1991a.

19. "Short, punchy claims are the most effective way to attract them [prescribing physicians] to the limited number of products about which they will be willing to spend some effort to absorb and evaluate details" (Cooper 1992, 156.).

20. For discussions, see Masson and Rubin 1985, Rubin 1991b, Rubin 1993, and Keith 1992.

21. See, for example, Benham 1972, 337; Steiner 1973, 19; Marvel 1976, 1033; Kwoka 1984, 211; Haas-Wilson 1986, 165; Farris and Albion 1980, 17; Albion and Farris 1981.

22. Only 36.4 percent of consumers "never" use the price of a prescription product as a basis for choosing a pharmacy (Wolfgang and Perri 1989). Greater provision of information would facilitate such price shopping between pharmacies, and more information would also allow price shopping between brands and drugs.

23. Based on the discussion in Rubin 1993. Also suggested by Calfee (1992).

References

Adams, David. 1992. "Pharmaceutical Advertising: Education versus Promotion." In *Promotion of Pharmaceuticals: Issues, Trends, Options,* ed. Dev S. Pathak, Alan Excovitz, and Suzan Kucukarslan, pp. 53–56. Binghampton, N.Y.: Pharmaceutical Products Press.

Albion, Mark, and Paul W. Farris. 1981. *The Advertising Controversy: Evidence on the Economic Effects of Advertising.* Boston: Auburn House.

Antman, Elliott M., Joseph Lau, Bruce Kupelnick, Frederick Mosteller, and Thomas C. Chalmers. 1992. "A Comparison of Results of Meta-analyses of Randomized Control Trials and Recommendations of Clinical Experts." *Journal of the American Medical Association* 268, no. 2 (July 8): 240–48.

Beales, Howard J., III. 1994. "Economic Analysis and the Regulation of Pharmaceutical Advertising." *Seton Hall Law Review* 24 (3).

Beales, Howard J., Richard Craswell, and Steven C. Salop. 1981. "The Efficient Regulation of Consumer Information." *Journal of Law and Economics* 24:491–539.

Beales, Howard J., and William C. MacLeod. "Experts' Assessments of Pharmaceutical Advertisements: A Critical Analysis." *Food and Drug Law Journal* 1995.

Benham, Lee. 1972. "The Effect of Advertising on the Price of Eyeglasses." *Journal of Law and Economics* 15.

Beckner, C. Frederick, III. 1993. "The FDA's War on Drugs." *Georgetown Law Journal* 82, no. 2 (December): 529–62.

Calfee, John E. 1992. "FDA Regulation: Moving Toward a Black Market in Information." *American Enterprise* 3, no. 2 (March/April): 34–41.

———. 1994. *Health Information in Advertising.* Washington, D.C.: American Enterprise Institute.

Chren, Mary-Margaret. 1992. "The Need for Guidelines About Pharmaceutical Promotions to Physicians." In *Promotion of Pharmaceuticals: Issues, Trends, Options,* ed. Dev S. Pathak, Alan Excovitz, and Suzan Kucukarslan. Binghampton, N.Y.: Pharmaceutical Products Press.

Chren, Mary-Margaret, and C. Seth Landefeld. 1994. "Physicians' Behavior and Their Interactions With Drug Companies." *Journal of the American Medical Association* 271, no. 9 (March 2): 684–89.

Comanor, William S. 1986. "The Political Economy of the Pharmaceutical Industry." *Journal of Economic Literature* 24:1178–1217.

Cooper, Richard M. 1992. "Marketing Violations." *Food and Drug Law Journal* 47:155–62.

Craswell, Richard. 1985. "Interpreting Deceptive Advertising." *Boston University Law Review* 65:658–732.

Farris, Paul, and Mark Albion. 1980. "The Impact of Advertising on the Price of Consumer Products." *Journal of Marketing* 44 (Summer).

Haas-Wilson, Deborah. 1986. "The Effect of Commercial Practice Restrictions: The Case of Optometry." *Journal of Law and Economics* 29 (April).

Ippolito, Pauline M., and Alan D. Mathios. 1990. "Information, Advertising and Health Choices: A Study of the Cereal Market." *Rand Journal of Economics* 21, no. 3 (Autumn): 459–80.

Jacoby, Jacob. 1994. "Misleading Research on the Subject of Misleading Advertising." *Food and Drug Law Journal.* In press.

Kaplar, Richard T., ed. 1993. *Bad Prescription for the First Amendment: FDA Censorship of Drug Advertising and Promotion.* Washington, D.C.: Media Institute.

Kazman, Sam. 1990. "Deadly Overcaution: FDA's Drug Approval Process." *Journal of Regulation and Social Costs* 1, no. 1 (September): 35–54.

Keith, Allison. 1992. "The Benefits of Pharmaceutical Promotion: An Economic and Health Perspective." In *Promotion of Pharmaceuticals: Issues, Trends, Options,* ed. Dev S. Pathak, Alan Excovitz, and Suzan Kucukarslan. Binghampton, N.Y.: Pharmaceutical Products Press.

Kessler, David, and Wayne L. Pines. 1990. "The federal regulation of prescription drug advertising and promotion." *Journal of the American Medical Association* 264:2409–15.

Kwoka, John. 1984. "Advertising and the Price and Quality of Optometric Services." *American Economic Review* 74.

Levine, Arthur. 1993. "The FDA's Expanding Control over Drug Promotion." In *Bad Prescription for the First Amendment: FDA Censorship of Drug Advertising and Promotion,* ed. Richard T. Kaplar, pp. 23–39. Washington, D.C.: Media Institute.

Mann, Charles C., and Mark L. Plummer. 1991. *The Aspirin Wars.* Boston, Mass.: Harvard Business School Press.

Marvel, Howard. 1976. "The Economics of Information and Retail Gasoline Price Behavior." *Journal of Political Economy* 84 (October)

Masson, Alison, and Paul H. Rubin. 1985. "Matching Prescription Drugs and Consumers: The Benefits of Direct Advertising." *New England Journal of Medicine* 313 (August 22): 513–15.

Mathios, Alan, and Mark Plummer. 1989. "The Regulation of Advertising by the Federal Trade Commission: Capital Market Effects." *Research In Law and Economics.* 12: 77–93.

Nelson, Philip. 1974. "Advertising as Information." Journal of Political Economy 82 (July): 729–54.

Peltzman, Sam. 1973. "An Evaluation of Consumer Protection Legislation: The 1962 Drug Amendments." *Journal of Political Economy* 81 (September): 1049–91.

———— 1981. "The Effects of FTC Advertising Regulation." *Journal of Law and Economics* 24 (December): 40348.

Pharmaceutical Manufacturers Association (PMA). 1993. *The Case for the Pharmaceutical Industry*. Washington, D.C.

Pharmaceutical Research and Manufacturers of America (PRMA). 1994 *The Case for America's Pharmaceutical Research Companies*. Washington, D.C.

Physicians' Health Study Group (PHSG), Steering Committee. 1989. "Final Report on the Aspirin Component of the Ongoing Physicians' Health Study." *New England Journal of Medicine* 321, no. 3 (July 20): 129–35.

Rubin, Paul H. 1990. *Managing Business Transactions*. New York: Free Press.

———. 1991a. "The Economics of Regulating Deception." *Cato Journal* 10 (Winter): 667–90.

———. 1991b. "The FDA's Prescription for Consumer Ignorance." *Journal of Regulation and Social Costs*, pp. 5-24.

———. 1992. "New Study on Drug Ads Misleads." *Wall Street Journal*, June 4.

———. 1993. "From Bad to Worse: Recent FDA Initiatives and Consumer Health." In *Bad Prescription for the First Amendment: FDA Censorship of Drug Advertising and Promotion*, ed. Richard T. Kaplar. Washington, D.C.: Media Institute.

———. 1994. "Are Pharmaceutical Ads Deceptive?" *Food and Drug Law Journal*.

Steiner, Robert. 1973. "Does Advertising Lower Consumer Prices?" *Journal of Marketing* 37:19.

Ward, Michael. 1992. "Drug Approval Overregulation." *Regulation* (Fall): 47–53.

Wilkes, Michael S., Bruce H. Doblin, and Martin F. Shapiro. 1992a. "Pharmaceutical Advertisements in Leading Medical Journals: Experts Assessments." *Annals of Internal Medicine* 116, no. 11 (June 1): 912–19.

———. 1992b. "In Response." *Annals of Internal Medicine* 117, no. 7 (October 1): 618–19.

Wolfgang, Alan P., and Matthew Perri, III. 1989. "Consumer Price Sensitivity Towards Prescriptions." *Journal of Research in Pharmaceutical Economics* 1 (4): 51–60.

4

FDA Regulation of
Medical Devices

Robert Higgs

We're a year and a half behind the rest of the
world, thanks to the FDA. We don't get
the...equipment we need to save lives.
—Keith Lurie, M.D.[1]

S ince World War II, medical devices have become increasingly
important in the practice of medicine for diagnosis, monitoring, and
treatment. More than 6,000 types are currently used, and the various
models and brands constitute a set with nearly 750,000 distinct elements
(Goldfarb and Wolfberg 1992, 35).

The device industry in the United States has grown rapidly and
now comprises some 13,000 (mostly small) firms employing about 280,000
workers. In 1993 the industry produced U.S. output valued at $43 billion,
or 46 percent of world production. About 23 percent of the U.S. output was
exported. The industry has been highly competitive internationally—it
generated a trade surplus of $4.7 billion in 1993. Including the output
produced in facilities operated abroad, American firms had a 52 percent
share of the world market (HIMA 1994, 40, 59, 68, 153).

Despite this apparent flourishing, participants in the U.S. device
business—producers, purchasers, medical practitioners, and the ultimate
beneficiaries, the patients—are deeply troubled. More and more device

firms are moving or considering moving their research and manufacturing facilities to Europe. Doctors, hospitals, and emergency medical services increasingly find that devices available elsewhere in the world are not available in the United States, and thousands of patients are suffering as a result.

The cause of these woes is evident: perplexing, costly, and time-consuming regulations promulgated and enforced by the FDA. An industry executive and former FDA official recently observed that "the pendulum may swing back eventually, but the pendulum at F.D.A. is more like a wrecking ball."[2]

In this chapter I consider how regulation intended to protect the public and enhance its health has become a wrecking ball. I describe how the FDA has gained greater legislative authority and imposed more sweeping regulations. I document how the agency has responded, especially during the past five years, to the demands of its congressional overseers and to scandals and shocking disclosures prominently featured by the news media. I describe how the device industry has been affected under the regime of Commissioner of Food and Drugs David Kessler, who took office at the end of 1990 and immediately adopted a more aggressive enforcement strategy. Finally, I describe where FDA regulation of medical devices stands today, focusing on some outstanding problems in the form and implementation of the current rules and their effects on producers, practitioners, and patients.

A Brief History of Device Regulation

Before 1976. The FDA first received authority to regulate medical devices when Congress enacted the Food, Drug, and Cosmetic Act of 1938 (FDC Act), which, as amended, remains the fundamental enabling statute. The act defined devices as "instruments, apparatus, and contrivances, including their components, parts, and accessories, intended (1) for use in the diagnosis, cure, mitigation, treatment, or prevention of disease in man or other animals; or (2) to affect the structure or any function of the body of man or other animals."[3] It prohibited all interstate dealings in "adulterated" or "misbranded" devices and authorized FDA to seize such devices by proceeding against them in federal courts.[4] "Adulterated" meant contaminated by filth, and "misbranded" meant that the labeling was "false or misleading in any particular."[5] Although the 1938 act required premarket approval of new drugs, it imposed no such requirement on devices. Therefore, the FDA could not prevent a device from coming onto the market; it could only ask a court to stop the continued sale or enjoin the production of a device already introduced into interstate commerce.[6] Under this authority, the FDA removed from the market scores of fraudulent or "quack" devices in the 1940s and 1950s (Hutt 1989, 105; Hutt and Merrill 1991, 735).

After World War II, as the device industry began to introduce many legitimate products of much greater sophistication and complexity—cardiac pacemakers, renal catheters, surgical implants, artificial vessels and heart valves, intrauterine contraceptive devices, replacement joints, and many other innovations—FDA regulators sought authority to require premarket testing of devices for safety and effectiveness, the same power they acquired over new drugs under the 1962 amendments to the FDC Act. Increasingly, device manufacturers were contesting the FDA's actions in the courts, and the regulators bridled at the need "to develop extensive evidence that would hold up during long legal proceedings to remove an unsafe device from the market."[7] Pushing the envelope, they resorted to a "regulatory fiction" that embraced the very notion Congress had rejected prior to enactment of the FDC Act in the 1930s and again while amending the law in 1962, namely, that devices are drugs for purposes of regulation.[8] During the 1960s, the FDA regulated intraocular lenses, soft contact lenses, weight-reducing kits, certain IUDs, and some *in vitro* diagnostic products as if they were drugs, requiring the manufacturers to provide satisfactory evidence of safety and effectiveness *before* placing the products on the market (U.S. FDA 1989, 1).

Enactment of a new device law did not occur, however, until public clamor had been magnified by shocking revelations (particularly the widely publicized flaws of the Dalkon Shield IUD), interest groups had exerted more pressure, and much political maneuvering had occurred. Finally, the Medical Device Amendments of 1976 were signed into law on May 28, 1976 ("Medical Device Regulation" 1976, 535–36; Hutt 1989, 110–12).

The 1976 Law. The new law conferred gatekeeping powers on the FDA.[9] It refined the old definitions, distinguishing a device from a drug by the condition that the former "does not achieve any of its principal intended purposes through chemical action within or on the body of man or other animals and...is not dependent upon being metabolized for the achievement of any of its principal intended purposes."[10] The FDA was required to classify devices into three groups.[11] Class I devices, the least risky, were made subject to general controls, including requirements that manufacturers keep certain records, file certain reports, and follow "good manufacturing practices" (GMP). Class II devices were made subject to the general controls and product-specific performance standards to be developed by the FDA in cooperation with panels of experts. Class III devices, the riskiest, were made subject to general controls and premarket approval (PMA). In all cases the objective was to "provide reasonable assurance of the safety and effectiveness of the device" while "weighing any probable benefit to health from the use of the device against any probable risk of injury or illness from such use."[12] Neither the statute nor the legislative history gave substantive guidance as to how the FDA should make the required classifications or weigh the risks against the benefits. Hence the law gave the regulators enormous discretion over life-and-death matters.[13]

Unless it were found "substantially equivalent" to a "preamendment device"—a product already on the market before passage of the Medical Device Amendments—any new device was automatically placed in Class III and thereby made subject to premarket approval. ("Transitional devices," those previously regulated as drugs, were also subject to premarket approval unless the manufacturer successfully petitioned for a reclassification.) Obtaining premarket approval required presentation of extensive test data, including the results of clinical trials, to satisfy the FDA that the product was safe and effective. The FDA could also require submission of PMA data from manufacturers of "old," or preamendment, Class III devices, but meanwhile the device could remain on the market. During the first 15 years after passage of the 1976 amendments, the makers of only 9 percent of the "old" Class III devices were required to submit PMA applications (U.S. House 1993, 8). Moreover, claiming a lack of resources, the FDA never created the performance standards for Class II devices required by the 1976 law.[14] Therefore, in practice the FDA's closest control over the manufacture of Class II and most Class III devices occurred through its GMP requirements and its regulation of new versions of "old" devices (U.S. House 1993, 7–9).

To sell a new version of a preamendment device, the manufacturer had only to file a premarket notification form 510(k). It would turn out that the great majority—about 98 percent—of products being introduced to the market arrived via the 510(k) route, so how the FDA dealt with these notifications would prove critical to the operation of the device industry (Merrill 1994, 68). A successful 510(k) had to show that the product had the same intended use as well as the same technological and descriptive characteristics as a "predicate device." In deciding whether the similarities were sufficient to establish "substantial equivalence," the FDA exercised great discretion and, as documented below, eventually made increasing and increasingly arbitrary demands for additional information, so the 510(k) evolved from a simple premarket *notification* to become in many cases an *application for premarket approval*. According to Peter Barton Hutt, former chief counsel at the FDA, the reviewers "sent back 510Ks with so many trivial, unimportant questions that they eventually became the same as a PMA."[15]

The FDA gained a variety of new enforcement powers from the 1976 amendments. It could ban a device. It could require manufacturers to notify users of risks or to repair or replace products or to give refunds.[16]

Aggrieved parties could seek judicial review of FDA actions, but the tables had been turned. Before, the FDA had been required to proceed through the courts before it could exercise its enforcement powers. Now, it could exercise its powers at will, and the offended party bore the burden of contesting the action in court.

  Congressional Oversight. After passage of the 1976 amendments, the FDA began to carry out its newly authorized activities with all deliberate speed, emphasizing the deliberateness more than the speed. As indicated above, the agency never did adopt standards for Class II products. Six years after enactment of the amendment, the House Subcommittee on Oversight and Investigations of the Committee on Energy and Commerce—both the subcommittee and the committee being chaired by John D. Dingell (D-MI)—found that the FDA had yet to complete the classification of devices and that it had not even begun the review of preamendment Class III devices as envisioned by the framers of the amendments (U.S. House 1993, 10).

  Thereafter, Dingell's subcommittee staff made monitoring and hectoring the FDA a substantial part of their daily grind. Their boss, one of the most powerful figures in Washington, enjoyed the publicity that came from haranguing FDA officials about their failings—"cavalier disregard for potential consequences" and "bureaucratic neglect for public health and safety that shocks the conscience"—while the crestfallen bureaucrats sweated under the glare of the television lights.[17] At FDA headquarters in Rockville, Maryland, Dingell's incessant inquiries and demands came to be dubbed "dingellgrams." The agency's answer was always the same: not enough staff, not enough money.[18]

  FDA officials sometimes expressed appropriate contrition. In an interview in 1986, John Villforth, director of the agency's Center for Devices and Radiological Health (CDRH), confessed that "many of the brickbats FDA has received for its implementation of the medical device law have been justified." But he insisted that not all device problems could be laid at the feet of the regulators. "With devices, the performance of the user is a major determinant of whether the patient is at risk. And the way you deal with that problem isn't necessarily through more regulations about how the equipment is manufactured. It's by working with those users—whether they're physicians, nurses, technicians or patients—to improve their understanding and their use of medical devices" ("Medical Device Amendments" 1986, 30–31). This was an astute observation but, unfortunately, one that the FDA would disregard as its regulatory activities evolved during the following decade.[19]

  Dingell's subcommittee displayed no interest in enhancing the capabilities of device users. The staff concentrated on the FDA's failure to carry out specific legislatively prescribed activities and the agency's alleged "unwillingness and/or inability to...take decisive enforcement action when device manufacturers could not, or did not, comply with regulations, and continued to market defective devices despite evidence of increasing numbers of serious or catastrophic device failures" (U.S. House 1993, 12). In pursuit of dragons for Chairman Dingell to be seen slaying, the staff made several case studies, accompanied by well-publicized hearings and reports.[20]

One of the most notable inquiries involved a defective artificial heart valve and gave rise to a 1990 report with the long, revealing title, "The Bjork-Shiley Heart Valve: 'Earn as You Learn,' Shiley's Inc's Breach of the Honor System and FDA's Failure in Medical Device Regulation." In its well publicized report of May 1993, the staff revisited this notorious example (U.S. House 1993, 12, 21–23). The extensive publicity generated by Dingell and his staff regarding the Bjork-Shiley valve clearly helped to tip the congressional balance toward approval of the Safe Medical Devices Act (SMDA), which was signed into law on November 28, 1990. This capped a series of legislative efforts over a period of seven years led in the House by Dingell and Henry A. Waxman (D-CA) and in the Senate by Ted Kennedy (D-MA), chairman of the Committee on Labor and Human Resources.[21]

Medical Device Reporting under the 1990 Law. The 1990 law requires every "device user facility" to report "information that reasonably suggests that there is a probability that a device has caused or contributed to the death of a patient...[or] to the serious illness of, or serious injury to, a patient...not later than 10 working days after becoming aware of the information." (Manufacturers had been required by regulation to make similar reports since 1984.)[22] Device user facilities include hospitals, ambulance services, surgical facilities, nursing homes, and outpatient treatment facilities. Death reports go directly to the FDA, illness or injury reports to the manufacturer of the suspect device.[23] Failure to report is punishable by a civil penalty assessed by the FDA with a maximum of $15,000 per violation and $1,000,000 for all violations adjudicated in a single proceeding.[24]

In view of the heavy penalties for failure to report, users need a clear definition of a reportable event. Yet the FDA put the burden of making the proper distinctions on the users themselves. According to FDA official Kay Chesemore, "facilities have to decide for themselves what constitutes a reportable event and what device or devices are implicated in the death or serious injury" (quoted in Goldfarb and Wolfberg 1992, 46). So the FDA, in effect, is saying to device users: You decide what to do, and later we'll decide whether to punish you for your decision. FDA inspectors have acted inconsistently in identifying reportable events and therefore violations of the statutory requirement (U.S. House 1993, 72). As late as May 1994, the FDA still had not clarified the requirement. Bryan H. Benesch, an agency enforcement official, confessed that "the lack of a final regulation has caused a great deal of confusion. Many people just don't know what they're supposed to do" (quoted in Burton 1994a).

The number of medical device reports (MDRs) increased from 27,883 in 1990 to 88,265 in 1993 (Burton 1994a), but it is doubtful that any benefits accrued as firms and institutions incurred the substantial costs of piling up these papers.[25] Annual costs of the MDR system were estimated at more than $42 million, but in responses to a three-state investigation between November 1992 and June 1993 most user-facility risk managers indicated that "SMDA [which requires the reporting] does not save lives" ("Device User FAcility" 1994, 17–19). Of the MDRs received in fiscal 1993, the FDA reviewed only 51.5 percent, so nearly half of them just lay in storage taking up space to no purpose. With the number of reports projected to reach 246,000 in 1995, the prospect looms of more wasted effort by the involuntary reporters.[26]

Because many illnesses, injuries, or deaths to which a device *may* have contributed actually result from operator error or improper maintenance rather than defects in the design or manufacture of the device, the reporting requirements in effect call for users who have made mistakes to report themselves to the feds.[27] Even though the statute forbids admission of the reports into evidence in civil actions,[28] device users understandably have feared that lawyers would use the Freedom of Information Act to secure the reports and "have a field day with medical device litigation" (Goldfarb and Wolfberg 1992, 45). According to Dr. Joel Nobel, the respected head of ECRI (a private testing organization whose publications are known as "the Consumer Reports of medical technology"), the reporting requirements create a "nightmare for health professionals. It's like throwing them in a tank of sharks" (quoted in Goldfarb and Wolfberg 1992, 45).

The fear is not misplaced, but personal liability litigation is only one of the risks. MDRs also invite abuse by incompetent, irresponsible, sensationalistic news media or opportunistic publicity seekers who call themselves consumer advocates, whose scurrilous pronouncements can cause irreparable harm. Grossly misleading journalistic exploitation of device reports has played an important part in leading the FDA to shut down entire companies, including the pioneering defibrillator maker Physio-Control Corporation, depriving patients of life-saving products.

In 1990 WRC-TV, an NBC affiliate in Washington, D.C., broadcast a program called "Fatal Flaws," highlighting the large number of MDRs by Physio-Control during the past six years and incorrectly interpreting the reports as evidence that the company's products must be defective.[29] In July 1992 WRC-TV aired a sequel to the "Fatal Flaws" program, noting that recently Physio-Control had stopped production. (The company had voluntarily done so in order to bring its procedures and paperwork into full compliance with new FDA regulations.) The next morning NBC's "Today Show" featured portions of WRC's program, exposing a national audience to what Jim Page, the editor of *Journal of Emergency Medical Services*, later called "a scurrilous 'hit piece'" (Page 1992, 5).

While Page was expressing regret that "opportunistic 'consumer reporters' have created unwarranted public anxiety about defibrillator safety," the political process passed quickly through its predictable phases. Newspapers and radio and television broadcasts across the nation repeated NBC's misinformation. Omnipresent consumer advocate Dr. Sidney Wolfe, head of Public Citizen's Health Research Group, demanded that the FDA clamp down on Physio-Control. Congressman Dingell, having already dispatched his staff to obtain the FDA's records on the company, voiced his usual deep concern for protecting the public health and told the television cameras that the FDA was "not doing its job."

Getting the hint, the FDA proceeded to make a harsh example of Physio-Control. After the intimidated company meekly signed an oppressive consent decree to avoid a sweeping injunction, it endured a series of administrative abuses and was not permitted to resume production of all its products until more than two years after the initial shutdown. Losing more than $70 million out of pocket and $100 million in sales during the down time, the company survived only by reaching into the deep pockets of its corporate parent, Eli Lilly & Co (Bowers 1994; Ludwig 1993). While customers waited for their defibrillator orders to be filled, heart attack victims died who might otherwise have been restored to life.

More New Regulatory Requirements. The SMDA also required creation of a tracking system for implantable and life supporting devices, augmented the data requirements for 510(k) applications, and repealed the 1976 law's requirement that performance standards be developed for all Class II products.[30] It imposed new reporting requirements on manufacturers, importers, and distributors, who must now inform the FDA of any removal or correction of a product undertaken to reduce a health risk or remedy a violation of regulations.[31] The new law gave the FDA authority to require product recalls and, for certain devices, postmarket surveillance.[32]

Importantly, the SMDA changed the character of the 510(k) procedure through which the great majority of new products had entered the market after passage of the Medical Device Amendments in 1976:

> The 510(k) process is no longer simply a notification, but
> an approval process. SMDA defines the terms "substan-
> tially equivalent" and "substantial equivalence," and

further stipulates that manufacturers submitting a 510(k) must wait to market a device until notified by FDA that their premarket notification has been found substantially equivalent. (U.S. FDA 1991, 3).

As documented below, this change in the 510(k) procedure led almost immediately to longer waiting times for manufacturers trying to place improved versions of their devices on the market.[33] Changes, no matter how small, might cause the product to be consigned to an indefinite stay in preapproval purgatory; manufacturers complained that their 510(k)s "seem to have fallen into a black hole" or "appear to be in eternal limbo." Firms therefore had a reduced incentive to make the minor improvements that, cumulating over time, could greatly improve the performance of their products.[34]

Also, as the FDA began to require more 510(k) applications to be supported by clinical trials, the distinction between a 510(k) and a PMA became progressively blurred.[35] Increasingly the FDA required both types of applicants to employ test protocols like those used in drug trials—not an easy requirement to satisfy, as some elements of a drug test (e.g., the placebo in the double-blind setup for drug testing) have no equivalent in a device trial.[36]

Finally, the 1990 law gave the FDA authority to impose civil penalties for all violations of the act up to $15,000 per violation and $1,000,000 for all violations adjudicated in a single proceeding.[37] While imposing such fines, the agency shall "take into account the nature, circumstances, extent, and gravity of the violation or violations and, with respect to the violator, ability to pay, effect on ability to continue to do business, any history of prior such violations, the degree of culpability, and such other matters as justice may require," but it "may compromise, modify, or remit, with or without conditions, any civil penalty which may be assessed."[38] In other words, the FDA may impose fines or not impose fines or change its mind about previous fines however it pleases, and whatever it does has statutory sanction.[39] In view of this practically unlimited discretion, industry representatives must have been dismayed when Ronald Johnson, director of the Office of Compliance of the FDA's Center for Devices and Radiological Health (CDRH) told them at a trade association meeting early in 1994 that imposition of civil penalties would become a "mainstay" of the agency's enforcement activities (*Medical Devices, Diagnostics and Instrumentation*, February 21, 1994, p. 3).

Passage of the Safe Medical Devices Act, which authorized such enormous additional regulatory power to be exercised by the FDA, ordinarily would have created a jubilant mood at the agency. But 1991 and 1992 ranked among the worst of years for the men and women of Rockville's regulatory colossus. Largely because of the scandal that captured the headlines in 1989, involving the bribery of several FDA officials by companies seeking expedited approval to market generic drugs, the agency was in crisis mode (Burkholz 1994, 47–62). Stung by pervasive criticism in Congress and the news media, FDA personnel were hunkering down, trying to protect themselves by avoiding anything, including product approvals, that might expose them to further censure.[40] As a staff report of Dingell's subcommittee observed, "Reluctant to make a decision that may result in criticism from FDA management or from the outside, some reviewers make endless requests for information from applicants to avoid doing so."[41] In addition, David Kessler had become commissioner in November 1990, his appointment itself being prompted by the scandal, and he was shaking up the organization with new appointments, reassignments, and a new agenda featuring unprecedented emphasis on aggressive enforcement and more stringent regulation (U.S. House 1993, 65–75; Gleason 1993, 13–15; Brimelow and Spencer 1993b, 108–110). The unsettled situation in 1991 and 1992 produced a "devastating slowdown in device clearances" and was aptly described as "chaos in US medical device regulation" (Kahan 1993, 21). In the midst of this turmoil, late in 1991, a new storm struck—the furor over silicone gel-filled breast implants.

Silicone Breast Implants. The implants have a long history. Their commercial marketing in the United States began in 1964. Since then, millions of women have used them. (Sources differ on exactly how many.) When the Medical Device Amendments were enacted in 1976, the implants continued on the market as grandfathered preamendment devices. From time to time FDA received complaints from users, and advisory panels raised some questions about the safety of implants, but the agency took no formal action to require data about them until 1988, when it finally classified them as Class III devices. The classification triggered a requirement that manufacturers submit evidence of safety and effectiveness for approval of PMAs not later than July 9, 1991 (U.S. House 1993, 26–27).

On December 13, 1991, a federal court awarded a plaintiff $7.3 million for injuries from connective tissue disease allegedly caused by the rupture of her Dow Corning silicone implants (Burton 1993). The news media—not to speak of the product liability lawyers—went into a frenzy.

> Never before has so much media and public attention been paid to medical devices—not during the debate that led to enactment of the 1976 Medical Devices Act, nor even during discussions over the provisions of the 1990 Medical Devices Act. Further, never before have there seemed to be so many

congressional hearings on medical devices. ...The saga of the Food and Drug Administration's (FDA) regulation of breast implants riveted media and public attention in late 1991 and early 1992. As the issue unfolded, literally dozens, if not hundreds, of stories appeared in the media.[42]

Appearances on popular TV talk shows by women blaming their implants for a variety of health problems fed the flames.

On January 6, 1992, Commissioner Kessler placed a 45-day moratorium on the sale of silicone implants. In March, Dow Corning announced it would no longer make such implants, leaving only two manufacturers, McGhan Medical and Mentor, in the business. In April, Kessler limited the use of silicone implants to patients enrolled in clinical trials, which would be open to any woman needing an implant for reconstruction but to only a limited number of women seeking breast augmentation.[43] All of these actions grew out of the media excitement exclusively, as the FDA had no compelling new scientific evidence—no large clinical trials of the sort it requires from manufacturers seeking to market new devices—to justify the new restrictions (Burton 1993; "Review of 1992" 1993, 3–24; FDA 1992, 1–2).

Later, thousands of lawsuits were consolidated in an enormous class action suit against the manufacturers of silicone gel–filled breast implants, and in 1994 a settlement was reached for $4.25 billion—the largest product liability award in history—to compensate plaintiffs for alleged injuries past and future (*Medical Devices, Diagnostics & Instrumentation*, April 18, 1994, pp. 8–9; Burton 1994c, b).

As the settlement was being approved, reports of epidemiological studies casting doubt on the plaintiffs' allegations began to appear. Neither a University of Michigan study nor a University of Maryland study found any association between implants and scleroderma. Mayo Clinic researchers found no association between implants and "rheumatoid arthritis, systemic lupus erythematosus, systemic sclerosis and other diseases of the connective tissue—all of which are among the autoimmune and other ailments cited during FDA and congressional hearings on implant safety." A Harvard Medical School study of 121,700 nurses "found no evidence that implants played a role" in causing scleroderma or several other diseases including lupus and rheumatoid arthritis. The editors of the *Wall Street Journal* opined that the federal court had made a "$4.3 Billion Mistake" (Kolata 1994; Schwartz 1994b; Bor 1994; "4.3 Billion Mistake 1994).

Undoubtedly, both the courts and the FDA had acted hastily on the basis of anecdotal and unsystematic evidence. While the courts might be forgiven, because cases before them have to be decided somehow, it is appropriate to hold the FDA to the same high scientific standards it requires of those subject to its regulation.   Undoubtedly the agency's moratorium early in 1991 and its subsequent restriction of implants to women participating in approved clinical studies helped to establish a climate of opinion in which the legal claims being made against silicone implants were viewed as well founded when in fact they were not.

Confronted with the epidemiological studies showing no evidence of a link between breast implants and any of the ailments allegedly caused by them, Bruce Burlington, head of the FDA's CDRH, said that the agency would maintain the course it had set before the studies were reported. The editors of the *Wall Street Journal* fumed: "This, after *billions* of dollars have been put up to pay off the plaintiffs' lawyers, after mastectomy patients were terrorized, and after companies and careers associated with the implants have needlessly washed over the falls" ("$4.3 Billion Mistake" 1994).

The Great Slowdown in the Approval Process.   From 1983 through 1990, the FDA received an average of about 80 PMAs per year and approved about 45.[44] In 1991 it approved only 27, which was fewer than in any year since 1979, when the approval process was just getting started (Olson 1993). In 1992 only 12 PMAs were approved, as the process ground nearly to a halt.   The following two years witnessed a rebound to 24 approvals in 1993 and 27 (according to preliminary data) in 1994, but these numbers were still only a little more than half the average for the period 1981-1990.[45]

In the late 1980s the average review time for FDA to approve a PMA was about 150 days. In 1991 it was 285 days, in 1992 it was 186 days (this average being misleading because six of the 12 approvals were licensing agreements with no data review), and in 1993 it was 437 days and still rising. Preliminary data for 1994 showed an average approval time of 604 days.   The total time elapsing from the applicant's filing until the approval of the application was substantially longer, nearly 800 days in 1993 and nearly 900 days in 1994. In extreme cases the process could eat up several years. C. R. Bard and Collagen filed a PMA for their Contigen incontinence device in March 1989. The FDA did not approve the application until four and a half years later. Jonathan Kahan, an attorney specializing in device law and regulation, attests that "there are numerous other examples of years of delay for devices which could have an important medical impact."[46]

The 510(k) process for "substantially equivalent" devices, where vastly more applications for marketing approval are processed, experienced a similar slowdown. In the 1980s the number of applications tended upward. By the early 1990s, manufacturers were submitting about 6,000 form 510(k)s per year. In 1993 there were 6,288 submitted and in 1994 there were 6,247 (according to preliminary data). FDA *decisions* on these applications also tended upward in the 1980s, reaching more than 6,000 per year in 1989 and 1990, then dropped to 5,367 in 1991 and further to 4,862 in 1992 and 5,073 in 1993. The number of 510(k)s *approved* fell every year from 1989 to 1992 before rebounding slightly in 1993, as shown by the following table:

Fiscal Year	510(k) Approvals
1989	4,867
1990	4,748
1991	4,294
1992	3,776
1993	4,007

In 1994 (according to preliminary data), under intense criticism for the slowdown, FDA made 7,101 510(k) decisions, including 5,463 approvals, but this rebound hardly indicated a reversal of trend. Even CDRH chief Bruce Burlington admitted that much of the 1994 resurgence had been achieved by what industry critics called "cherry picking," or attending to the easiest cases first, and by temporarily diverting personnel from other tasks (Schwartz 1994a).

As the approval rate dropped in the early 1990s, the 510(k) backlog at the FDA grew much longer. At the end of fiscal year 1991, there were 2,291 applications awaiting disposition; in 1992 there were 3,951; in 1993 there were 5,157; and in 1994 (according to preliminary data) there were still 4,303. The average active review time increased from less than 90 days in the 1980s to 102 days in 1992 and 182 days in 1994. Counting the time the average application spent "on hold," awaiting the arrival of additional information requested by an FDA reviewer, the total time spent waiting for clearance of a 510(k) reached 214 days in fiscal year 1994—up more than 100 percent in three years.

Early in 1993 someone leaked to the *Wall Street Journal* the FDA's internal record of 510(k)s pending more than 90 days, and the newspaper published a striking graph of the monthly figures on its editorial page. In November 1991 only two 510(k)s were pending more than 90 days. The number then grew exponentially, reaching 713 a year later. The *Journal's* editorialists linked the growing backlog to "the aftermath of the Kessler-Congress jihad against breast implants" ("Kessler's Devices" 1993). Six months later the number of overdue 510(k)s had reached about 1,400 ("FDA Outlines Steps" 1993), and late in 1993 some 2,000 before its reduction by the agency's "cherry picking" in 1994 (Schwartz, 1994a). The buildup of the huge backlog in 1992 and 1993 was the development that led bewildered applicants to speak of a "black hole" and "eternal limbo."

In August 1994, at the International Medical Device Congress in Salt Lake City, FDA's Susan Alpert, director of the Office of Device

Evaluation, presented a graph showing "a steady decline since fiscal year 1988 in the percentage of 510(k)s acted on within 90 days. While approximately 80% met the deadline in 1988, only about 60% did so in 1991 and 40% in 1993" ("FDA-Industry Interaction" 1994, 3). A study by the Health Care Technology Institute (HCTI), based on a sample of applications classified by the year of their submission, showed even greater deterioration—only 23 percent of the 510(k)s submitted in 1993 received a decision within 90 days—before a turnaround in 1994 that left the agency's completion rate for reviews still far below its pre-1992 level (HCTI 1994b, 8).

When the approval slowdown had become apparent to everybody and industry executives appealed to Congress for relief, Representative Dingell sent FDA an angry letter in the summer of 1992, calling for an end to the "unconscionable" paralysis. At Rockville, agency personnel were dumbstruck. After all, Dingell's unrelenting criticism of them for approving applications too readily had been a major reason for their increased deliberateness. As recently as March and June of 1992, Dingell had held hearings to flagellate them for regulatory lapses. Reminded of his apparent inconsistency, Dingell replied that FDA had overreacted.[47]

More Aggressive Enforcement. The FDA is a full-service government bureaucracy. Within broad and often vague statutory limits, it makes the rules, monitors compliance without inconveniences such as search warrants and, with wide discretion, punishes those it finds guilty—it is promulgator, police, judge, jury, and executioner all rolled into one.

The agency's actions are subject to formal judicial review, but aggrieved parties go to the courts only as a last resort. Apart from the likelihood that they will lose in a court of law, where judges usually countenance a wide range of agency action,[48] they will eventually lose in any event, because as long as they remain in business they will be subject to the agency's enormous and ill-defined regulatory powers, and the agency will take its revenge sooner or later. Its vindictiveness is notorious. Kim Pearson, publisher of the *Food & Drug Insider Report*, "found that 84% of companies polled in 1991 reported declining to file a complaint against the FDA for fear of retaliation."[49] After drug company executives blew the whistle on corrupt FDA officials and precipitated the generic drug scandal in 1989, FDA rewarded them by trying to drive them out of business with repeated inspections—in which "violations" of GMP regulations can always be found—and long delays in approving their products for marketing.[50] An FDA official reportedly said, "We have depended on the ability to selectively target companies…and to issue findings without fear of being second-guessed by some tinhorn judge."[51] Separation of powers is not a popular constitutional doctrine at agency headquarters in Rockville; indeed, the Constitution, if it is considered at all, is evidently viewed as a nuisance.[52]

Before Kessler took command of the agency, it tended to use its powers with some sense of restraint and some appreciation of the value of expediting the marketing of innovative products of great benefit to the public. According to Richard A. Merrill, the FDA's chief counsel from 1975 to 1977, "the first managers of the FDA's new Bureau of Medical Devices believed that regulators, inventors, and manufacturers should work cooperatively. Most did not share the suspicion of manufacturers' motives held by many FDA field inspectors and some reviewers of drugs. And they took seriously the claims by architects of the 1976 amendments that regulation should not discourage the development of new devices" (Merrill 1994, 59). In the eyes of some observers these attitudes had fostered "inefficient, and often ineffective, enforcement practices" (U.S. House 1993, 65). Agency critics had often faulted it for going too lightly on the firms it regulated.

With Kessler's arrival, aggressive enforcement moved to the top of the agency's agenda. The new commissioner delegated more enforcement authority to the district offices and encouraged them to use it. Compliance officials encouraged a philosophy of "act now, talk later."[53] The district offices responded by finding more GMP violations, issuing more warning letters, and taking a variety of other enforcement actions at an increased rate, as documented below. Says former FDA chief counsel Hutt, "The more enforcement actions, the more FDA employees showed they were protecting the public health" (quoted in Porter, 1994, 19).

The correlation, however, was spurious. There was no evidence that products had become any safer as a result of the agency's stepped-up compliance program.[54] But if the public did not actually benefit, Commissioner Kessler did, as his "get tough" policy resulted in much publicity portraying his fearless protection of health and safety (for example, see Stout and Gutfeld 1993; Schwartz 1993).

Companies must admit to their facilities and respond to the questions of FDA inspectors who appear with a form 482 notice of inspection. However, inspectors frequently appear without a 482 and conduct inspections, during which they may obtain evidence used in subsequent criminal prosecutions. Companies that admit the inspectors without a 482 are deemed to have waived their Fourth Amendment right against illegal search and seizure notwithstanding the absence of a search warrant. In the wake of the generic drug scandal, inspectors have searched more diligently for criminal violations.[55]

FDA inspectors proceed on the assumption that the company being inspected is violating the law; their attitude "resembles that of a police detective's toward suspected felons."[56] Said an official of the Office of Compliance, "We're cops and that's part of the cop psychology" (quoted in Burkholz 1994, 58). This attitude predisposes the inspectors to be

unreasonable—it really is outrageous that the government should routinely treat the creators of highly beneficial and often life-saving products
as suspected felons—and during the past four years, under increased
goading by their superiors, they have become more unreasonable. "Companies report an increasing and often inexplicable change in regulatory
attitude by device inspectors. The new attitude is characterized by greater
hostility and less communication."[57]

Moreover, many of the inspectors are ill-trained or wholly unquali-
fied to deal with the technologies they scrutinize.[58] "FDA now takes
aggressive enforcement action, yet lacks the controls and training to avoid
inconsistent or arbitrary decisions."[59]

In general, the FDA has failed to clarify for companies precisely
what actions constitute compliance. The result has been "an enforcement
program that is perceived by industry as disorganized, inconsistent, and
often inappropriately harsh" and "a confused, demoralized industry no
better able to comply with the law" (U.S. House, 1993, 66; Porter 1994, 21).

There is no way to measure exactly how much the FDA has
increased its enforcement activity during the past few years. The agency's
own reports give conflicting figures on the number of various kinds of
enforcement actions taken, and even with consistent data no single index
tells the whole story. Issuance of regulatory/warning letters more than
doubled, increasing from 235 in fiscal 1991 to 548 in 1992, 543 in 1993, and
(according to preliminary data) 549 in 1994—a reflection of the unleashing
of the district offices.[60] Nearly 70 percent of the warning letters pertain to
GMP violations, which are often the sort of transgression visible only to an
inspector who wants to see it.[61] Despite the name, "good manufacturing
practice" violations usually have nothing to do with actual manufacturing
or with the quality of the product that reaches the customer; they almost
always consist of failures to fill out countless forms in the minute detail that
only a bureaucrat could care about.[62] The period 1992–1994 also witnessed
an average of 34 seizure actions annually. In addition, in the three fiscal
years combined, the FDA's general counsel sought 21 injunctions, brought
seven criminal prosecutions, and assessed five civil penalties against
device manufacturers. Virtually all industry sources agree that FDA not
only has stepped up enforcement activities markedly but has taken these
actions in a way that seems more focused on punishing the industry than
working with it to ensure the rapid delivery of safe and effective products
to the market. The 1993 report of Dingell's Subcommittee on Oversight
and Investigations concluded, "FDA enforcement practices have demoralized and perplexed the medical device industry" (U.S. House 1993, 85).

Perhaps the most perplexing enforcement initiative was FDA's
adoption of the "Reference List"—known in industry as the "Black
List"—in April 1992. The FDA places on the list companies for which

inspectors have identified "serious uncorrected or unresolved violations" of GMP or (in about 5 percent of cases) other regulations. It then refuses to process applications from listed firms for 510(k)s and certain PMA Supplements. Every company issued a warning letter is put on the list, but others also may be.[63] The number of companies on the list quickly grew to about 600 (U.S. House 1993, 217; Kahan 1994b, 26). The FDA gives no notice to a company when it is placed on the reference list, and the criteria for removal are vague. The Health Industry Manufacturers Association (HIMA) has questioned the FDA's legal authority to link GMP requirements with agency determinations of a product's "substantial equivalence" to a preamendment device. It also protests that the way in which the FDA uses the list denies the listed companies due process of law, because it does not conform to the procedural requirements for notice-and-comment rule making ("HIMA advocates clarity" 1993, 9; "Hearings for Device Firms" 1994, 12–14). Suppose, for example, that a company is mistakenly placed on the list or mistakenly not removed from it and then finds that its 510(k) applications go nowhere. Such a firm has entered a bureaucratic twilight zone and has no way to know how it got there or how to escape. While firms want to be informed of their placement on the Reference List, they do not want the list to be made public, not even through Freedom of Information Act disclosures, fearing that publicity of inclusion on the list might damage their reputation with customers or attract product liability suits. HIMA has sought to have the FDA formally promulgate a rule to bind itself from releasing the names of listed companies ("HIMA advocates clarity" 1994, 9; "Hearings for Device Firms" 1994, 14). On September 2, 1994, the law firm Hyman, Phelps & McNamara filed a citizens' petition urging the revocation of the Reference List because it "deprives those companies [listed] of rights to adequate notice and opportunity to be heard, property rights, and liberty interests guaranteed by the Constitution" ("FDA 'Reference List' Violates" 1994, I&W 7–8).

Early in 1994 the FDA began to employ a devastating new sanction—Kahan calls it "the nuclear weapon in the FDA arsenal"—the complete shutdown of *several* facilities of a multiplant company. Not content to require correction of cited deficiencies or to close only the facility where violations have been observed, FDA now goes after the entire product line(s) of a corporate entity, excepting only the production of spare parts and servicing of products already in use. In this way, says CDRH's compliance chief Johnson, the agency seeks to rectify a "corporate attitude" of noncompliance, to compel corporate managers to "look at their overall corporate philosophy" or "corporate culture" (quoted in Kahan 1994a, 6–7). Remarkably, the FDA has not even alleged that deaths or serious injuries have occurred because of the GMP violations at issue in these firms. The agency is effectively saying to them: We don't like your attitude; and until we do, we are not going to permit you to sell your products in the United States.

Each of the three companies with multiple facilities shut down early in 1994—Puritan-Bennett, National Medical Care (NMC), and Siemens Medical Systems (SMS)—chose to sign a consent decree rather than fight the FDA's request for a court injunction. Both NMC and SMS pledged to bring into GMP compliance not only their U.S. facilities but all their foreign facilities manufacturing certain products for sale in the United States. SMS, which had U.S. sales of $1.8 billion in the fiscal year ending in September 1993, stood to lose 8 percent of its U.S. sales (about $144 million) from the shutdown, which extended to only some of the firm's product lines. This is a hefty penalty for what SMS President Robert Dumke described as "primarily procedural and record-keeping issues— not the safety or effectiveness of our equipment" ("Siemens Shipment Suspensions" 1994, 5). Puritan-Bennett, a much smaller firm than SMS, undertook to bring one of its two closed plants into compliance with GMP and MDR (medical device report) regulations but decided to abandon a plant in Boulder, Colorado, explaining; "It is no longer economically feasible for this relatively small operation to continue trying to satisfy expanding regulatory requirements." The plant's 100 workers had to look for new jobs, and the consumers who would have benefited from the product, a portable home ventilator, had to turn to less satisfactory alternatives. Puritan-Bennett indicated that it would transfer its manufacturing of the ventilator to Ireland and continue to sell it overseas ("Puritan-Bennett Closing" 1994, I&W 7–8).

Effects of FDA Regulation on the Device Industry

The men and women of the U.S. medical device industry display remarkable forbearance of the regulations under which they labor. I have yet to find a single one who favors abolishing the FDA. They are willing "to do almost anything that the Agency wants, so long as it is clearly stated, with minimal room for interpretation" (U.S. House 1993, 84). Yet no matter how forgiving they may be, they can go only so far. Unless they can get their products to market, keep their costs low enough, and predict future regulatory burdens with some confidence, they cannot continue to operate.

The recent changes of FDA policies and conduct have increased the device firms' costs of research and development, product approval, manufacturing, and postmarketing surveillance of product performance. Unfortunately, industry managers perceive no commensurate increase in safety and efficacy, that is, no substantial additional benefit for consumers of their products and hence no basis for raising product prices enough to offset the increased costs. In the estimation of venture capitalist Robert

Daly, "The new regulations and delays mean adding $10 million to $20 million to a company's budget, and several years until the device gets to market. At that rate, most [venture capital] deals don't make sense."[64] Increased costs mean that some investments are no longer expected to generate a satisfactory return, some innovations are no longer worthwhile to develop, and ultimately some patients will suffer and die as a result.

The FDA now requires many more device firms to conduct clinical trials similar to those required of drug firms. Before beginning a trial, a company must gain FDA approval, known as an Investigational Device Exemption (IDE), for its plan to conduct the tests. Like PMAs and 510(k)s, these applications lately have become subject to extended and often inexplicable delays. A consultant who wrote to Dingell's oversight subcommittee in 1993 asked the legislators to "imagine the frustration a clinician/researcher feels when a faceless bureaucrat, often without medical training or any familiarity with the clinical environment, produces an endless stream of unrealistic questions effectively casting a 'no' vote on a research application" (quoted in U.S. House 1993, 80).

Venture capitalists increasingly have responded to this situation as did Grant Heidrich of the Mayfield Fund: "We counsel our companies, 'Don't screw around with the F.D.A; let's move these trials to Europe where there's a reasonable process'" (quoted in Fisher 1993). Indeed, U.S. device firms increasingly are shifting their trials to Europe, even though they must still meet all FDA requirements to get approval to sell their products in the United States. Said Rob Michiels, president of Interventional Technologies, which manufactures an innovative catheter used to clear arteries, "By the time we're approved in the U.S., that product will have been available in Europe on the free market for three to four years" (quoted in Fisher 1993). David Summers, chairman of American Biomed, a small company that also manufactures catheters, echoes Michiels: "We're having to move out of the United States. We just can't take it anymore" (quoted in Fisher 1993).

Heightened Uncertainty and Lack of Communication. If the FDA simply took longer to approve products, manufacturers could at least factor the increased delay into their planning, minimizing the harm to their programs for developing and marketing new or improved products. But FDA's approval times are not just longer; they are also more variable and more difficult to fathom. Said John Wright, vice president for engineering at Ultracision, "It's the inconsistency and the impossibility of predicting when you are going to hear from them that makes planning impossible" (quoted in Seybert 1994). Commissioner Kessler, on the other hand, evidently thinks the unpredictability of his agency's actions, especially their enforcement actions, is a good thing—keeps the companies on their toes (U.S. House 1993, 81, fn. 139).

Many producers complain that the approval process tends to be frustratingly reiterative. Said Phil Schein, president of CDX Corporation, a manufacturer of noninvasive monitoring devices, "You spend a lot of time doing a lot of work, trying to meet all the requirements. And yet, once you've met the requirements, they come back and say, 'You need to do this'" (Seybert 1994). In a Gallop survey (1994, 4) of 58 medical device company executives in 1994, 57 percent of the respondents affirmed that the FDA had applied guidance instructions retroactively to their approval submissions. Elsewhere a manufacturer observed that "the delays are often over issues of form rather than scientific substance. Once the FDA takes a position, reason and logic have little influence over the outcome of decisions."[65] In a 1993 survey of its readers by the trade publication *Devices & Diagnostics Letter*, 85 percent of the respondents said requests for data on submissions were reaching them late in the review cycle, 63 percent said such requests were arriving 90 or more days after filing, and 48 percent characterized the FDA's requests as "unreasonable." One respondent commented that the FDA had asked the company "'to re-prove well accepted scientific principles' and when some questions did not make sense, 'the reviewer would not talk to me to clarify' them" (quoted in "No Improvement" 1993, 5).

Nothing frustrates device companies more than the FDA's refusal to communicate and the cryptic nature of the communications they do get. For example, plant inspectors cite firms for GMP violations, expressed in very general terms, but refuse to provide any guidance as to how the violations ought to be remedied. The agency places firms on the Reference List but refuses to spell out exactly what a firm must do for removal from the list. Injunctions and consent decrees list violations with references to vaguely worded sections of the FDC Act and the *Code of Federal Regulations*, leaving firms puzzled as to precisely how they must tweak the nuts and bolts of their production process to comply.[66]

To divine what they should do to get past the enforcers or the product reviewers, firms often hire consultants who specialize in regulatory compliance. In consent decrees, the FDA routinely requires that a firm, at its own expense, hire such a consultant to certify compliance before the FDA itself will reconsider the firm's compliance status. Surprise: such consulting firms are staffed by former FDA employees.[67]

In May 1992, when FDA personnel were feeling especially beleaguered, the Office of Device Evaluation (ODE) adopted a policy on telephone communications between product reviewers and manufacturers that can only be described as paranoid. The announcement of the new rules noted that the ODE intended "to avoid the kind of circumstances that arose within the generic drug program," where the bribery scandal had occurred in 1989. The rules described in excruciating detail what sorts of calls could be made or accepted and required a detailed recording of all calls.[68] This hyper-restrictive policy held industry applicants virtually incommunicado. Minor problems that might have been resolved easily by a telephone conversation went unresolved for weeks or months.

Companies lingered in limbo, unable to make financial or production plans or to inform customers about the scheduling of future deliveries. The FDA was essentially telling applicants; Don't speak unless spoken to; otherwise we'll ignore you. Meanwhile the fate of businesses and the care of ill and dying patients were effectively being decided in the silence.[69] During Physio-Control's two-year travail of complete or partial shutdown, for example, the company's employees complained bitterly and often that they could not get the FDA to respond to their telephone messages. As company president Richard Martin told the *Wall Street Journal*, "Weeks can go by without our phone calls being returned."[70]

In February 1993 the ODE adopted a somewhat less restrictive policy on phone contacts with industry, but the improvement was slight, and device company personnel continued to voice a variety of complaints about the poor quality of their communication with the regulators ("No Improvement" 1993, 4–5).

Like many others, Physio-Control's Martin also complained that in dealing with FDA, "The process is absolutely arbitrary" (quoted in Bowers 1994). Just how arbitrary was dramatically illustrated by an experiment conducted by R S Medical, a small firm that manufactures muscle stimulators. When the FDA denied a 510(k) application and rescinded an earlier approval, R S Medical reapplied twice—under its own name and separately under the name of a consulting firm retained to act as a front. The disguised application sailed through the approval process, but the firm's own was rejected. The FDA was not amused when the company revealed what it had done. R S Medical then went to court seeking an order to restrain the agency from blocking its sales. Amazingly, the company won. In December 1993, on the recommendation of Federal Judge John Primomo, the court permanently enjoined FDA from stopping R S Medical's sales. Judge Primomo noted "the agency's seemingly biased attitude towards R S Medical" and concluded that "a substantial likelihood exists that the reasons given for the denial of substantial equivalence findings were a mere pretext." His opinion catalogued a number of "arbitrary and capricious" actions by the regulators, including their differing treatment of the two identical applications, which the judge called a "blatant inconsistency" (quoted in Bowers 1994, "FDA's 'Arbitrary and Capricious' Denial" 1993, 9–11).

Capital Flight. As noted above, few firms challenge the FDA in court. Doing so makes sense only for those who are desperate and will not survive unless they receive judicial protection. Even those (very few) who win in court cannot expect to survive the agency's subsequent retribution; a court victory can only buy time for the firm to minimize its losses. The only effective escape is to flee the country, which more and more device firms reluctantly are choosing to do. According to analyst Daniel Lemaitre, "There isn't a company that isn't thinking of moving its research and development, and its manufacturing, overseas" (quoted in Jereski 1993).

Several recent surveys confirm that increasing numbers of device firms are leaving or considering leaving the United States. In a 1992 survey by attorney Jeffrey Gibbs of representatives of 168 firms attending regulatory affairs seminars, almost 60 percent of the respondents indicated that in the future they would introduce new products outside the United States first, and almost 75 percent were planning to manufacture at least some of their products abroad. They gave the difficulty of U.S. product approval as the reason for shifting their production overseas ("FDA Driving" 1992, 13).

Early in 1994 HIMA, the largest medical device trade association, reported the findings to date of three of its own industry surveys, which indicated an increasing movement offshore. In a survey encompassing 98 companies, the regulatory environment ranked highest as a "decision factor in expected international expansions and new operations"; 40 percent of the respondents gave FDA regulation as the most important reason for moving abroad.[71] In a Strategic Business Decisions Survey, HIMA found that companies "cited the regulatory climate here as their top reason for planning to shift to overseas operations in the next four years— double the number that cited it for the earlier period [1991–1993]" (HIMA 1994b, 4). In December 1994 a HIMA official confirmed that the shift of operations to Europe represented a trend and not a transitory action.[72]

In April and May 1994 the *Minneapolis Star Tribune* conducted a survey of medical device firms in Minnesota, where many such firms do business. The newspaper secured responses to its questionnaire from 148 firms in device manufacturing or research and development. The survey showed that firms selling Class III devices—the most heavily regulated ones—had 7 percent of their personnel employed overseas five years ago and 12 percent currently, but expected to have 16 percent in 1999. Respondents complained of "costly and cumbersome regulation" in the United States, citing this as a "leading reason for the investing abroad before investing at home" (Meyers 1994).

In November 1994 Medtronic, a Minnesota firm that describes itself as "the world's leading therapeutic medical device company," announced plans to move the headquarters of its Corporate Ventures organization to Europe, explaining that the relocation was being made "because of pressures related to the current unpredictability of regulatory and reimbursement processes in the United States" (Medtronic news release, Minneapolis, November 22, 1994).

In June 1994 the American Electronics Association (AEA) announced the results of a survey, conducted by the Gallop Organization, of 58 U.S. medical device companies. Of the firms surveyed, 40 percent said they had reduced the number of U.S. employees because of FDA delays; 29 percent said they had shifted investment spending offshore; and 22 percent said they had relocated jobs to overseas facilities. Bob DeHaven, vice chairman of AEA, warned that the U.S. medical device industry faces decline "unless the FDA regulatory process is re-engineered" (AEA news release, Washington, D.C., June 23, 1994).

Data on capital outflows confirm the survey findings and related reports. From 1989 to 1991, U.S. medical technology firms invested almost the same amount abroad each year, in the range of $321–333 million. Then in 1992, when the FDA abruptly made its enforcement and approval policies more onerous, capital outflow jumped more than 200 percent to $993 million. HIMA (1994a, 76–77) interprets the increase as a verification that "as the FDA approval process has become more burdensome and slowed, U.S. companies have moved to establish overseas facilities at a much faster rate." Given that during 1991–1993 Europe was wallowing in its worst recession since the 1930s and that labor and other variable costs there may exceed U.S. levels, it would appear that the recent movement offshore represents a regulatory push out of the United States rather than an economic pull toward Europe.

Finally, the stock market registered unmistakably the reversal of prospects for the U.S. device industry produced by the changes in FDA behavior which reached their full force in 1992. Goldman Sachs has constructed an index of the average stock price of a composite of publicly traded medical device companies relative to the S&P 500. From its base of 1.0 in 1989, the index rose steadily to a peak of about 4.0 late in 1991. It then began to fall steadily, losing about half its value in the following two years.[73] Clearly, under the new regime at the FDA, the device industry's financial future looks much bleaker not only to venture capitalists but also to investors in established firms.

Concluding Observations

The preceding account has been rather detailed because, in regulatory matters, the devil really is in the details. But with regard to the FDA, the devil is in the basic principles, too. The enabling statutes that undergird the FDA's device regulations are essentially misguided. They rest on a paternalistic foundation that is inconsistent with the maximization of consumer welfare and the preservation of a free society (see Higgs 1994a, b).

They also reflect a naive faith in central planning that flies in the face of all experience by empowering the FDA to act as a Politburo for an industry in which 13,000 firms produce more than 6,000 heterogeneous products in facilities scattered across the United States and around the world. Little wonder if the simple legal categories and one-size-fits-all rules only create bewilderment for those who bear their brunt. As Dr. Nobel aptly remarks, "On the face of it, the legislation may make sense to amateurs. But if you have experience and knowledge in this field, it is foolish as well as costly" (Nobel 1993, 15).

The FDC Act, as amended, gives broad and ill-defined discretion to the FDA. Public choice theory leads us to expect that a regulatory agency equipped with such discretion will use it to promote the interests of government officials rather than the public interest.[74] The evidence shows quite plainly that the course of device regulation has been driven by the personal and political motives of both congressional overseers and FDA officials, as they have sought to continue in office and to enhance their power and perquisites while reacting to the shocking revelations of sensationalistic, incompetent, and irresponsible news media and, in turn, making complaisant media the mouthpieces for their propaganda.[75]

Perfection: The Wrong Standard. At the root of the public's misplaced support of strict FDA regulation of medical devices is a widely accepted two-part misconception: (1) that medical devices should operate perfectly and (2) that when they do not, Congress and the FDA should do something to make them operate perfectly.[76] This is a specific instance of the public's general desire for complete security and for the federal government to intervene whenever risks of harm become evident. The public wants the impossible and has faith that the government can deliver it. In the prophetic words of Bertrand de Jouvenel, the government "comes to be looked on as a sort of living umbrella, and its proliferation is received not only with complacency but with enthusiasm" (de Jouvenel [1945] 1993, 391).

Unfortunately, medical devices cannot be made to operate perfectly. They can be made safer, but making them safer is costly. The lower the risk level already achieved, the greater the cost of the next increment of risk reduction. Eventually, making a device even a little bit safer can be achieved only at prohibitive cost. Long before a device has been made as safe as technically possible, it will have become so expensive to produce that nobody will be willing to pay for it. Sad to say, on this side of heaven, people must make trade-offs. If we cannot achieve perfection and we are unwilling to bear the cost of approaching it very closely, we are necessarily left with devices that will sometimes fail. This outcome is nobody's fault. Human contrivances cannot be made to work perfectly—and should not be even if it were possible, because the costs would far outweigh the benefits.

How Large Is the Risk? Though products cannot be made perfect, they can be made amazingly good. Many American medical devices, even some that have been heavily criticized in the news media, have compiled very impressive performance records. Even the notorious Bjork-Shiley heart valve worked satisfactorily in 99.5 percent of its uses.

Physio-Control's defibrillators, rabidly attacked by the news media and Public Citizen's Health Research Group (HRG), have compiled a superb record. From 1985 through 1991, the FDA received 630 MDRs involving a death *associated* with use of the company's products (Schoch 1992). Recall that submission of an MDR does not signify that the product actually *caused* the death, although the news media and so-called consumer advocates commonly embrace the fallacy that it does. To make the most outrageously unjustified case against Physio-Control's products, suppose that everyone of the 630 deaths did result from a defibrillator failure. Is the implied rate of failure high? Consider that more than 100,000 of the company's defibrillators were in use, being used on average at least 10 times per year (Schoch 1992; Physio-Control Corporation press release, Redmond, WA, July 7, 1992). Therefore, for the seven-year period the rate of fatal failure is 630 divided by more than 7,000,000, or less than 0.00009. In other words, the products functioned properly in more than 99.991 percent of their uses, even though many of them were used in abusive environments by firefighters or paramedics who treat the defibrillators roughly in the field. As documented above, most MDRs for defibrillators have been shown by follow-up investigations to be caused by operator error or improper maintenance rather than equipment failure. Therefore, the actual failure rate is less than half of that hypothetically constructed above, which means that the products actually performed flawlessly in more than 99.995 percent of their uses, which is to say that they failed less than once in every 22,222 uses. These are the same products that HRG, in a widely publicized letter to David Kessler on August 26, 1993, described as "Physio-Control's deadly devices." In the letter HRG urged Kessler to initiate *criminal prosecution* of Physio-Control "for its widespread and ongoing noncompliance with GMP and MDR violations."[77]

Other cases of alleged poor product performance also look rather different when placed in the context of the number of products involved. Pfizer subsidiary Infusaid, for example, received the first civil penalty imposed by the FDA under the new authority granted by the SMDA, a fine of $290,000 for GMP violations and for marketing an altered device without prior FDA approval ("Infusaid Assessed $290,000" 1993, 4). The company had attracted the FDA's attention when it recalled 3,923 drug infusion pumps about which it had received 10 complaints involving product failure and patient injury. Ten failures were surely regrettable, but the rest of the products—that is, 99.75 percent of them—evidently had performed properly.[78]

In April 1994 the FDA issued a warning letter to U. S. Surgical Corporation for failing to report 15 cases of malfunctioning of its surgical stapler. The letter said that in three cases the malfunctioning *may* have caused injury to a patient. A company representative said U. S. Surgical had not reported the incidents because they occurred when users improperly loaded staple cartridges into the device, not because of faults in the device itself ("U.S. Surgical Receives" 1994). But suppose the product *had* failed, causing injury, in the three instances. The company has sold more than a million of the devices since 1991 ("U.S. Surgical Receives" 1994). Assuming that they have been used during this period on average at least three times, the injury-causing failure rate is 3 divided by more than 3,000,000, or one in more than a million, which implies a successful use rate in excess of 99.9999 percent. The works of man can scarcely come any closer to perfection than that.

Large Costs, Small Benefits. American consumers have suffered. They have had to pay the higher prices caused by the higher costs that manufacturers must bear to comply with ever-expanding FDA regulations. More important, they have had to wait for extended periods to gain access to new or improved products, and as a result they have experienced much unnecessary suffering, many of them dying prematurely. The FDA can cause many deaths by a single regulatory action, and it does so commonly. For example, Dr. Nobel's "best guess" is that the FDA's recall of the Bunnell infant jet ventilator in 1992 caused "anywhere from 10 to several hundred infant deaths."[79] Dr. Richard Cummins, a leading authority on defibrillation, believes that the FDA's shutdown of Physio-Control might have caused a thousand deaths (statement on ABC's *20/20* television program, August 12, 1994).

Finally, consumers have suffered, and will continue to suffer, perhaps most of all from an invisible effect of the FDA's costly and unsettling regulations, namely, the loss of innovations that under less hostile conditions would make available new products of great benefit. Asks manufacturer Bert Bunnell, "Can anyone deny the development and introduction of new, more advanced devices is stifled, obstructed and—as time goes by—destroyed before it even starts?"[80] In the circumstances, it is remarkable that the device industry continues to operate as well as it does—another example, no doubt, of what Adam Smith had in mind when he spoke of there being "much ruin in a nation."

Unfortunately, no appreciable offsetting benefits exist. As Nobel concludes, the medical device legislation "has not made devices safer" (Nobel 1993, 15). The protection the FDA claims to have produced for the public has been largely illusory. Consider that

Neither the FDA nor ECRI can say with certainty how many deaths or serious injuries result annually from medical devices. Difficulties exist with differentiating device-related error from user-related error. Factoring in the contribution of a patient's own illness to death or injury only compounds the difficulty, experts say.[81]

How can the FDA claim to have improved a situation if it has no firm idea what the situation was in the first place or is now?

In May and June 1994, the Gallop Organization (1994, 38) surveyed 58 executives of U.S. medical device companies. Among the questions asked was, "What effect, if any, have new FDA policies had upon product safety?" Seventy-nine percent of the respondents said "no effect," 14 percent said the policies improved safety "somewhat," and just 2 percent (i.e., a single respondent) said the policies improved safety "significantly."

HIMA correctly asserts that "there is no evidence which indicates that products available in these major overseas markets [but still unapproved by FDA for sale in the United States] are any less safe than products available in the United States" (U.S. House 1993, 237). Reporters Tom Hamburger and Mike Meyers echo the point: "Although patients in these countries may be taking risks Americans don't take, there's little evidence that they are harmed."[82] Isolated examples that the FDA might adduce in support of its actions cannot overturn this general conclusion.

The lack of demonstrable benefits from FDA device regulation is hardly surprising. Even if the FDA did not exist, normal market incentives combined with the terrors of product liability litigation are more than sufficient to encourage manufacturers to produce *reasonably* safe and effective products (see Higgs 1993, 59–69). The emergency care providers, hospital administrators, and medical practitioners who purchase the bulk of the devices have experience and knowledge and access to ample expert information about products from reliable sources such as ECRI, TUV Product Service, and a variety of trade and professional publications. They fervently desire to help, not hurt, the patients they serve, and their reputations depend on their success in doing so. In short, neither device purchasers nor patients need the FDA's "help." The agency's intrusion has clearly created far more cost than benefit for virtually all parties except the politicians, bureaucrats, consultants, and lawyers who have enjoyed the benefits of office and income associated with the operation of an extensive legal and regulatory regime.[83]

In Dr. Nobel's words, "the basic legislative concepts and methods prescribed by Congress have been wrong" (Nobel 1993 14). The entire undertaking—root and branch—will not bear informed and disinterested scrutiny. As Nobel suggests, it has plausibility to amateurs but not to people who really understand the workings of the technology, the industry, and the market. All in all, it is best characterized as an egregious example of the politically motivated pretense of protection that proves viable only when propped up by government propaganda and coercive force. Can anyone seriously suppose that the FDA would survive if it had to operate as a firm in the free market for information?

Reflecting on the slipping away of America's technological leadership in medical devices to competitors in Europe and Japan, Dr. Robert Hauser, a cardiologist at the Minneapolis Heart Institute and former chief executive of Cardiac Pacemaker, muse, "It's incredible what we're doing to ourselves" (Hamburger and Meyers 1994a). This is a common but misleading formulation. In truth, "we" are not deliberately harming ourselves; Congress and the FDA are the guilty parties, the former more so than the latter. Citizens who support the official actions are either ill-informed, ideologically misguided, or devoted to somehow gaining personally from a process in which the great majority of people lose. Unfortunately, some strategically situated parties, such as the congressional committee staff members, most of the so-called investigative reporters on television, and nearly all so-called consumer advocates, suffer from all three disabilities simultaneously.[84]

The Current Outlook. Criticisms leveled at the FDA in 1993 and 1994 by representatives of industry, a few prominent reports in the news media, and, most important, Dingell's subcommittee prompted the agency to initiate several changes ostensibly designed to speed product approvals and clarify regulations. With the possible exception of quicker product approvals financed by user fees—should Congress ever authorize them—none of the recent initiatives promise to diminish significantly the burdens on the device industry and hence the harm to the ultimate consumers of the products, the patients (Kahan 1995, 19–22). Nor do the most recent measures create any genuine benefits for consumers. The near-term prospect remains as it has been for the past several years—long delays in getting products to the market, reduced investment, reduced innovation, and industry flight to the less hostile regulatory climate of Europe.

Notes

1. Lurie as quoted in Hamburger and Meyers 1994a. Dr. Lurie, a member of the faculty at the University of Minnesota, is the developer of a simple chest pump widely used throughout the world for more effective cardiopulmonary resuscitation but forbidden by the FDA for sale or even testing in the United States.

2. "Wrecking ball" statement by Kshitij Mohan, vice president for scientific affairs in the Hospital Business Group at Baxter International. See also "FDA driving" 1992, 13; "US manufacturers" 1994, 1; Fisher 1993, p. C1.

3. 52 U.S. Stat. 1040 (June 25, 1938), at 1041.

4. Ibid., at 1042, 1044. At the time, the FDA was in the Department of Agriculture, and the statutory language actually gave authority to the Secretary of Agriculture. The secretary delegated the authority to the FDA.

5. Ibid., at 1049, 1050.

6. A 1934 draft bill defined devices as drugs and subjected them to the same legal requirements, but this definition did not survive congressional reworking of the statutory language. See Foote 1978, 106–7.

7. Quotation from "Medical Device Regulation" 1976, 535. See also Hutt and Merrill 1991, 736.

8. Hutt 1989, 102–8. A bill introduced in 1961, and in every succeeding Congress until passage of the Medical Device Amendments, required a premarket showing of safety and effectiveness for devices. Congress chose not to include this provision in the important 1962 drug law amendments. See Foote 1978, 108; Hutt and Merrill 1991, 743.

9. 90 U.S. Stat. 539 (May 28, 1976). In the statutory language, the powers are vested in the Secretary of Health, Education, and Welfare. In practice, the powers are delegated to the secretary's subordinate, the Commissioner of Food and Drugs, who heads the FDA.

10. Ibid., at 575.

11. A year before the law was enacted, the FDA established 14 panels and began classifying devices. Hutt (1989, 111), who was the FDA's chief counsel at the time, notes that "these administrative initiatives by the FDA concerned members of Congress and their staff, who argued that the FDA should have waited for specific statutory authority before acting. Nevertheless, they served a very important function, i.e., keeping pressure on Congress to enact the new legislation." See also Foote 1978, 114.

12. 90 U.S. Stat., at 541. Foote (1978, 112) observes that for devices employed by health professionals, "the House Report makes clear that evaluation of safety and effectiveness information of these devices should be with reference to their suitability for use by professionals rather than laypersons...[and take into account] whether the device will be used primarily in hospitals or solely in the home."

13. Foote 1978, 115, 116, 121, 123. In the latitude allowed the regulators,

this statute was typical. As Hutt and Merrill (1991, 20) observe, "FDA has enjoyed unusual freedom to adopt and revise regulatory approaches."

14. Hutt (1989, 112–13) maintains that "development of performance standards for class II devices…was not made mandatory and was left to the sole discretion of the FDA according to agency priorities and resources." Others disagree. See Hutt and Merrill 1991, 772.

15. Hutt as quoted in "International Markets" 1994, 13. In 1988 FDA officials noted that a House bill requiring clinical test data for 510(k) applications "would merely codify current agency policy" in effect since June 1986 in selected cases (*Congressional Quarterly Almanac 1988*, p. 320). Agency reviewers believed that "the law provides great latitude in assessing whether 510(k) applications are substantially equivalent to a predicate device" (U.S. House 1993, 39).

16. 90 U.S. Stat., at 560–64.

17. U.S. House 1983, iii–iv, quoted in Foote 1986, 517. Dingell used almost identical phrasing while berating the FDA at hearings in May 1987. See *Congressional Quarterly Almanac 1988*, p. 320.

18. *Congressional Quarterly Almanac 1988*, p. 320; Burkholz 1994, 13–14, 47–48; Brimelow and Spencer 1993a, 118. The staff of Dingell's oversight subcommittee did not accept the FDA's standard excuse, commenting that "the FDA's inability to manage its resources effectively is well known to those who have monitored the Agency for any length of time" (U.S. House 1993, 15; see also pp. 41 and 43).

19. In 1992 Jim Page (1992, 91), the editor of *Journal of Emergency Medical Services*, assailed the FDA for "concentrating their attention on manufacturers rather than on the much bigger problems of user training and operator error."

20. "A hearing is not a hearing in Washington, D.C. unless the media shows up, and a function of any congressional investigatory staff is to maximize publicity" (Pines 1992, 577).

21. 104 U.S. Stat. 4511 (1990); "Legislative History" 1990; "New Regulations" 1990. In 1988 the House had passed a bill similar to the SMDA, sponsored by Dingell and Waxman (chairman of the Dingell committee's Subcommittee on Health and Environment), but the Senate did not act on it. The administration opposed the bill because, among others things, it would "inundate the FDA with data which would require a staggering amount of effort to process and analyze" (*Congressional Quarterly Almanac 1988*, p. 319).

22. Manufacturers must report to the FDA by telephone not later than 5 calendar days and in writing not later than 15 working days after receipt of the information (49 *Fed. Reg.* 36326-36351, September 14, 1984, at 36349).

23. 104 U.S. Stat., at 4511.

24. Ibid., at 4527. Again, the statute actually vests the powers in the Secretary of Human Services, but in practice the secretary delegates them to the Commissioner of Food and Drugs.

25. Burke 1991, 42, citing an ECRI advisory that expresses doubt "whether such massive amounts of data will add much in the way of meaningful information."

26. *Medical Devices, Diagnostics & Instrumentation*, March 21, 1994, p. 5. Dr. Nobel describes the user reporting scheme as "a horribly flawed concept" and presents it as a "bizarre example" of how "Congress passes legislation that demands safe devices and micromanages the process by prescribing in great detail unworkable, inefficient methods" (Nobel 1993, 8).

27. Jack Olshansky calls user error "unquestionably the most frequent contributor to MDRs" (Olshansky 1990, 506).

28. 104 U.S. Stat., at 4512.

29. ECRI issued a press release calling "Fatal Flaws" misleading and inflammatory and urging the public to ignore the show (ECRINet SYSTEM NEWS, August 7, 1992). Medical investigations have shown that "most MDRs for defibrillators involve operator errors in performance or maintenance rather than device errors or failures" (Newman 1994, 17). See also medical literature cited in Newman 1994, 20, notes 16–18.

30. 104 U.S. Stat., at 4514–19. As indicated above, legal authorities had disputed whether the Class II performance standards were required or merely permitted by the 1976 amendments.

31. Ibid., at 4520.

32. Ibid., at 4520–23.

33. Larry Pilot, Washington counsel for the Medical Device Manufacturers Association, commented that the 510(k) application process "has spun out of control. People talk about a 'drug lag' in the US. This is worse; we're going to become a laughing-stock" (quoted in "MDMA focuses" 1994, 11).

34. Kahan 1992, 13; "U.S. rethinking" 1993, 13, 15; "510(k) decision-making" 1994, 20–21; U.S. House 1993, 51: "There is apparently no system for differentiating between applications for new devices, and manufacturing changes for currently marketed devices. ...[Manufacturers] cannot improve their competitive position in the market if they cannot make rapid changes in the manufacturing process of devices....[I]nspectors are...indicating that the manufacturer has committed a violation by failing to file a new 510(k) application, even when the manufacturer considers the manufacturing change to be minor."

35. Merrill (1994, 64) reports that "FDA's past practice...had resulted in requests for clinical data for just over 5 percent of all 510(k) notifications. Since 1990, however, that rate has tripled to 15 percent."

36. Kahan 1994b, 23–25; Kahan 1994c, 8–9. Merrill (1994, 48, 62–63)

notes that the FDA's regulation of devices "seems to be moving inexorably toward the 'drug model.'"

37. 104 U.S. Stat., at 4526-4528.

38. Ibid., at 4527.

39. When the FDA first used its authority to impose civil penalties by fining Infusaid, a Pfizer subsidiary, $290,000 in late 1993, it was rewarded by the demagoguery of Congressman Ron Wyden (D-OR), who assailed the FDA for going too lightly on the company (*Medical Devices, Diagnostics & Instrumentation*, February 28, 1994, pp. 3–5). In contrast, the FDA levied a whopping $1,580,000 civil penalty on a small company, Lexicor, and its founder, Michael Hickey, in September 1993. The fine amounted to twice the firm's 1993 revenue and led it to devote more than half its staff time to compliance with FDA regulations. Said Lexicor's lawyer, "This is a good, cheap PR lesson to scare the hell out of other small businesses" (quoted in Bowers 1994).

40. Thottam 1993; U.S. House 1993, 225–30 (draconian controls over telephone communication of FDA personnel with industry).

41. U.S. House 1993, 45 (see also pp. 46–48). According to Jonathan Kahan (1992, 13–14), "the drastic increase in the amount of data being requested by reviewers…is a reflection of an effort by reviewers to ensure that there is sufficient data in the 510(k) to withstand scrutiny by internal FDA auditors and outside parties, including the Inspector General and Congressman John Dingell. Reviewers fear accusations of not properly assuring the safety and efficacy of devices and react by 'papering the file.' …[T]here is no clear guidance at this time as to what data are needed to support 510(k) notices for the various types of devices. Each 510(k) sponsor is shooting at a moving target with the reviewer having complete discretion as to what data to request in connection with each filing." See also Ingersoll 1992, which remarks on the irony that "one of the main reasons for the slowdown [heavily criticized by Dingell in 1992 and 1993] was intense pressure from prominent lawmakers, including Rep. Dingell himself."

42. Pines 1992, 571. See also "Medical device industry" 1992, 12: "This adverse publicity quickly spilled over to encompass all medical devices and now the media are ready to report any controversial story involving medical devices."

43. This discrimination made no sense on safety grounds, and some observers attributed it to Kessler's close connections with Naderites and left-liberal feminists. See Brimelow and Spencer 1993b, 110.

44. The data for these years have been compiled by Mary Olson. I read them from graphs in her unpublished paper (1993). I am grateful to Dr. Olson for a copy of her paper. The years mentioned in this section are federal government fiscal years.

45. Unless otherwise noted, these data and those that follow are drawn

from *Medical Devices, Diagnostics & Instrumentation,* January 3 and July 25, 1994; *Clinica,* March 17, 1993, and March 28, 1994; and data provided to me by the Health Industry Manufacturers Association (courtesy of Gabrielle Williams).

46. Kahan 1994b, 24. See also the anguished letters from Drs. Marcus, Wilkinson, and O'Neill and the list of 49 important products awaiting U.S. approval (but already being sold abroad) reprinted in U.S. House 1993, 152–57, 231–33, 238–43.

47. Ingersoll 1992; U.S. House 1993, 17 (on the March and June hearings). The latter report, which I cite frequently, was the product of Dingell's anomalous phase of concern about the harm to industry and patients caused by the FDA's overzealous regulation. See "Industry sways" 1992.

48. Kahan 1994a, 8: "litigation with the FDA is a very costly and risky adventure." Hutt and Merrill (1991, 20) note that administrative discretion is "characteristic of the regulatory process, but FDA has enjoyed unusual freedom to adopt and revise regulatory approaches."

49. Brimelow and Spencer 1993a, 116. Attorney Dvorah A. Richmond has highlighted "the industry's unwillingness to fight as one reason for FDA's increasingly aggressive actions, giving the FDA the ability to bully the industry into submission" (quoted in Porter 1994, 21). Dr. Joel Nobel (1993, 23) warns industry executives that those who oppose the regulators "will become a permanent member of CDRH's hit list. The agency does maintain long-term vendettas against specific companies. How do we know this? Because FDA's staffers tell us in chapter and verse how disgusted they are by the practice."

50. Burkholz 1994, 48–62. Peter Barton Hutt, former general counsel at the FDA, attests that "the broad mantle of GMP enforcement can be used for other agency agendas" (quoted in "International Markets" 1994, 12).

51. Brimelow and Spencer 1993a, 117 (quoting *Food & Drug Insider Report*).

52. "Of all the government regulatory agencies created by Congress, the FDA has been the most expansive and the most punitive in inhibiting speech" (Seigenthaler 1993, xiii). It seems to me that the FDA routinely violates the rights of citizens as guaranteed by not only the First Amendment of the Constitution but also the Fourth, Fifth, and Tenth Amendments. Evidently the root of this evil is, as usual, the Supreme Court's expansive reading of the Commerce Clause. (See Shapiro and Tomain 1993, 488–93.) In their 1,354-page *Food and Drug Law,* Hutt and Merrill (1991) devote only a few pages to constitutional issues, confined to Fourth Amendment questions (pp. 1102–11). Here (pp. 1104–7) federal judges have taken the seemingly absurd position that citizens entering into a type of business "long subject to close supervision and inspection" or "perva-

sively regulated" thereby forfeit their Fourth Amendment protection!

53. "Compliance and Enforcement" 1993, 32. Damaska (quoted here) had recently retired as director of the Division of Compliance Operations in the Office of Compliance and Surveillance at the FDA's Center for Devices and Radiological Health.

54. Dingell's oversight subcommittee observed in a 1993 report that notwithstanding the increase in enforcement actions, "there is no evidence that medical device companies have greater compliance problems now than they ever have had in the past" (U.S. House 1993, 82).

55. "SOPs Needed" 1994, 22. For court decisions and other materials relevant to the FDA's inspection authority, see Hutt and Merrill 1991, 1102–21.

56. Porter 1994, 19. Hutt and Merrill (1991, 20) observe, "Many FDA employees have devoted their lives to gathering proof of statutory violations in preparation for court enforcement proceedings, and this adversary experience has engendered suspicion of regulated firms. This suspicion has in turn produced a desire to devise requirements that cannot be escaped or subverted."

57. U.S. House 1993, 83. According to device lawyer Kahan, "It has become more difficult to deal with FDA enforcement actions and negotiate a reasonable resolution to problems" (quoted in "Honour lost" 1992, 17). Kathryn Gleason (1993, 14) notes that the FDA has singled out certain companies, such as Physio-Control, to make examples of, approaching them "with a predisposition to remedy compliance concerns through injunctive or other forms of formal legal action rather than through voluntary compliance."

58. Says Nobel (1993, 7), "Beyond incompetent, they are stubborn."

59. U.S. House 1993, 88. On "untrained inspectors who can not, or will not, distinguish between 'significant' and 'nonsignificant' GMP violations," see ibid., p. 66, and details on pp. 69–70 and 73.

60. For 1991 and 1992 my source is "The Enforcement Story," an internal FDA document issued by the Office of Enforcement in the Office of Regulatory Affairs; for 1993 and 1994 it is the Office of Enforcement as reported in data sheets provided to me by the Health Industry Manufacturers Association.

61. "International Markets" 1994, 12, quoting lawyer Peter Barton Hutt for the 70 percent estimate. Ronald Johnson, director of the Office of Compliance and Surveillance, confirmed that GMP had been made "the central focus of our enforcement programme" (quoted in "FDA's regulatory priorities" 1994, 27).

62. For GMP "the FDA simply issued a series of broadly-defined and wide-ranging regulations that provided its reviewers and inspectors with maximum flexibility, and largely failed to follow up with detailed guide-

lines to better advise industry" (U.S. House 1993, 74). According to Dr. Nobel (1993, 22), whose opinion in this regard deserves more weight than anyone else's, "there is no known relationship between GMP paperwork and actual product performance in the field."

63. "The Reference List: What It Is and What It Is Not," enclosure sent to all registered medical device companies with letter from Ronald M. Johnson, Director, Office of Compliance and Surveillance, January 21, 1993, reprinted in U.S. House 1993, 215–18.

64. Quoted in Jereski 1993, 48. See also the statements of venture capitalist Chuck Hadley in HIMA 1994c, 5. Even before the recent changes, venture capitalists felt immense frustration with FDA regulation. See the observations of venture capitalist Jack Olshansky in Olshansky 1990.

65. Quoted in U.S. House 1993, 81. See also pp. 77–84 for many variations on this theme.

66. For example, *United States of America v. Physio-Control Corporation*, Complaint for Injunction, U.S. District Court, Western District of Washington, July 21, 1992, pp. 3–5.

67. Trade publications often carry advertisements such as that for the Medical Device Inspection Company, which appeared in *Medical Industry Executive*, April 1993, p. 32. The ad gives prominent notice that the firm is "Staffed by Former FDAers & Industry Experts."

68. ODE Integrity Memorandum No. 192-2, May 1, 1992, reprinted in U.S. House 1993, 225–30.

69. Not returning phone calls extended beyond product approval reviewers. Enforcement officers in the district offices often behaved similarly. See U.S. House 1993, 46–47, on "Communications with Industry."

70. Quoted in Bowers 1994. Similarly, Medtronic spokesman Dick Reid said that when company employees tried to find out why their implantable defibrillator had not been approved during the 17 months elapsing after the FDA's advisory panel had recommended its approval, they "found phone inquiries to be futile" (quoted in Ingersoll 1992).

71. "U.S. manufacturers" 1994, 1; "Preliminary Findings, Strategic Survey," compilation provided to me by HIMA (courtesy of Gabrielle Williams).

72. Interview with Matthew S. Gallivan, HIMA associate vice president for Europe and the Americas, December 9, 1994.

73. Values taken from a chart reproduced in "Innovation threatened" 1994, 15. See also HCTI 1994a, 5.

74. For an introduction to public choice analysis, see Mitchell and Simmons 1994.

75. Porter (1994, 21) notes that in the news media "FDA is most often portrayed as a crusader protecting the unwary public from greedy, negligent medical product manufacturers."

76. Porter 1994, 19, citing observations of Bunnell.

77. Besides receiving the usual serious notice in the respectable news media, this letter prompted a lurid story in a tabloid: "Code Blue—It's an Outrage—Faulty heart zappers killed 322," *National Examiner*, September 28, 1993. Publicizing its demands for criminal prosecution of medical device manufacturers is a common antic of HRG. See, for example, "FDA Urged" 1992, 1.

78. For a comparative perspective on rates of device failure, consider that "as many as 30% of hospitalized patients may experience an adverse drug event (ADE) during their hospital stay" and "fatal ADEs are expected in approximately 0.31% of hospitalized patients (60,000 to 140,000 patients annually) in the United States" (Classen et al. 1991, 2847).

79. Nobel 1993, 10–13. This FDA action was so manifestly harmful that some 60 hospitals simply ignored the order and continued to use the Bunnell ventilator, which had no effective substitute and without which some babies would surely die. The episode was described on ABC's "20/20" television program, August 12, 1994. The FDA's actions were savaged by Nobel (1993, 12), who said, "I simply do not have strong enough words to express my anger over this."

80. Quoted in Porter 1994, 19–20. In addition to sources cited above, see Littell 1994. Littell is executive director of Health Care Technology Institute.

81. Burke 1991, 42. Hospital administrators quoted by Burke say that equipment breakdown is "a rare occurrence" and "medical device problems are infrequent."

82. Hamburger and Meyers 1994a. I have found *no* systematic evidence.

83. Hutt (1989, 113), one of the architects of the FDA's device regulation, offered a quite different evaluation: "FDA has succeeded in exerting sufficient regulatory control to protect the public health, while at the same time avoiding over-regulation that would discourage medical device innovation and harm the public health." One wonders whether Hutt would reaffirm this 1989 judgment today.

84. For a superb account of the role played by so-called consumer groups, explicitly in relation to FDA drug regulation but equally applicable to device regulation, see Beckner 1993, 548–49.

References

Beckner, Frederick, III. 1993. "The FDA's War on Drugs." *Georgetown Law Journal* 82 (December).

Bor, Jonathan. 1994. "Studies weaken disease-implant link." *Seattle Times* (reprinting *Baltimore Sun*), October 25.

Bowers, Brent. 1994. "Entrepreneurs Find FDA Can Make or Break Them." *Wall Street Journal,* April 12.

Brimelow, Peter, and Leslie Spencer. 1993a. "Food and drugs and politics." *Forbes* 152 (November 22).

———. 1993b. "Just call me 'Doc.'" *Forbes* 152 (November 22).

Burke, Marybeth. 1991. "Hospitals wary of interpretation of medical device reporting law." *Hospitals,* October 20.

Burkholz, Herbert. 1994. *The FDA Follies.* New York: Basic Books.

Burton, Thomas M. 1993. "Breast Implants Raise More Safety Issues." *Wall Street Journal,* February 4.

———. 1994a. "Law Concerning Medical Devices Is Often Ignored." *Wall Street Journal,* May 2.

———. 1994b. "U.S. Judge Clears Breast-Implant Accord." *Wall Street Journal,* September 2.

———. 1994c. "Women With Breast Implants Receive Court Deadlines for Joining Settlement." *Wall Street Journal,* April 20.

Classen, David C., et al. 1991. "Computerized Surveillance of Adverse Drug Events in Hospital Patients." *Journal of the American Medical Association* 266 (November 27).

"Compliance and Enforcement—Past, Present, and Future: An Interview with William H. Damaska." 1993. *Medical Device & Diagnostic Industry* (July).

de Jouvenel, Bertrand. [1945] 1993. *On Power: The Natural History of Its Growth.* Reprint (original French edition 1945), Indianapolis: Liberty Fund.

"Device User Facility Civil Penalties Will Go into Effect." 1994. *Medical Devices, Diagnostics & Instrumentation,* May 23.

"FDA driving device manufacturers out of the US?" 1992. *Clinica* 532 (December 23.)

"FDA-Industry Interaction in Guidance Development Welcomed." 1994. *Medical Devices, Diagnostics & Instrumentation,* August 22.

"FDA Outlines Steps To Speed Up Reviews Of Medical Devices." 1993. *Wall Street Journal,* June 25.

"FDA 'Reference List' Violates Constitutional Due Process Protections." 1994. *Medical Devices, Diagnostics & Instrumentation,* September 19.

"FDA urged to prosecute Siemens-Elema." 1992. *Clinica* 514 (August 19).

"FDA's 'Arbitrary and Capricious' Denial of R S Medical's 510(k)s." 1993. *Medical Devices, Diagnostics & Instrumentation,* August 16.

"FDA's regulatory priorities for 1994." 1994. *Clinica* 585 (January 10).

Fisher, Lawrence M. 1993. "Frustration for Medical Innovators." *New York Times*, June 30.

"510(k) decision-making process should remain with manufacturer." 1994. *Medical Devices, Diagnostics & Instrumentation*, July 4.

Foote, Susan Bartlett. 1978. "Loops and Loopholes: Hazardous Device Regulation Under the 1976 Medical Device Amendments to the Food, Drug and Cosmetic Act." *Ecology Law Quarterly* 7.

———. 1986. "Coexistence, Conflict, and Cooperation: Public Policies Toward Medical Devices." *Journal of Health Politics, Policy and Law* 11 (Fall).

"The $4.3 Billion Mistake." 1994. *Wall Street Journal*, June 17.

Gallop Organization. 1994 (June). "Survey of Medical Device Manufacturers Concerning the Strategic and Economic Impact of the Federal Regulatory Process."

Gleason, Kathryn. 1993. "U.S. Enforcement Trends in the '90s." *Clinica Supplement* (October).

Goldfarb, Bruce, and Doug Wolfberg. 1992. "Feds Focus on Medical Devices." *Journal of Emergency Medical Services* 17 (July).

Hamburger, Tom, and Mike Meyers. 1994a. "Losing the Edge." *Minneapolis Star Tribune*, June 26.

———. 1994b. "Losing the Edge: Minnesota medical firms say they must export technology, jobs." *Minneapolis Star Tribune*, June 27.

Health Care Technology Institute (HCTI). 1994a. "Trends in Venture Capital Funding for the Medical Device Industry." *Insight* (quarterly update prepared by HCTI), March.

———. 1994b. "Understanding FDA Medical Device Review Statistics." *Insight* (quarterly update prepared by HCTI), September.

Health Industry Manufacturers Association (HIMA). 1994a (January). *The Global Medical Device Market Update: Markets for Medical Technology Products*. HIMA Pub. 94-1.

———. 1994b. "Member Surveys Track Regulatory, Business Actions." *Primus* (monthly newsletter of HIMA) 4 (May).

———. 1994c. "Venture Capitalists Still Investing, But Selectively." *Primus* (monthly newsletter of HIMA) 4 (May).

"Hearings for Device Firms Facing Placement on FDA's 'Reference List.'" 1994. *Medical Devices, Diagnostics & Instrumentation*, February 28.

Higgs, Robert. 1993. "Allocation of Risks Associated with Medical Goods." *Journal of Private Enterprise* 9 (Summer).

———. 1994a. "Banning a Risky Product Cannot Improve Any Consumer's Welfare (Properly Understood), with Applications to FDA Testing Requirements." *Review of Austrian Economics* 7.

———. 1994b. "Should the Government Kill People to Protect Their Health?" *Freeman* 44 (January).

"HIMA advocates clarity of Reference List procedures." 1994. *Clinica* 592 (February 28).

"Honour lost to tougher device enforcement." 1992. *Clinica* 500 (May 13).

Hutt, Peter Barton. 1989. "A History of Government Regulation of Adulteration and Misbranding of Medical Devices." *Food Drug Cosmetic Law Journal* 44.

Hutt, Peter Barton, and Richard A. Merrill. 1991. *Food and Drug Law: Cases and Materials.* 2nd ed. Westbury, N.Y.: Foundation Press.

"Industry sways Dingell to its side." 1992. *Clinica*, September 9.

"Infusaid Assessed $290,000 Civil Penalty for Unapproved Modifications." 1993. *Medical Devices, Diagnostics & Instrumentation*, November 29.

Ingersoll, Bruce. 1992. "FDA Attacked For Holding Up Medical Devices." *Wall Street Journal*, September 9.

"Innovation threatened by lack of venture capital?" 1994. *Clinica* 601 (May 2).

"International Markets Embrace Novel Devices." 1994. *In Vivo* (June).

Jereski, Laura. 1993. "Block that innovation!" *Forbes*, January 18.

Kahan, Jonathan. 1992. "The changing 510(k) process." *Clinica* 529 (December 2).

———. 1993. "US medical device regulation in 1992." *Clinica* 533 (January 6).

———. 1994a. "Corporate-wide medical device compliance initiatives." *Clinica* 612 (July 18).

———. 1994b. "1993—A roller coaster ride for US industry." *Clinica* 585 (January 10).

———. 1994c. "Use of clinical data in support of US and EU device clearances." *Clinica* 604 (May 23).

———. 1995. "US medical device regulation in 1994." *Clinica Review* (January).

"Kessler's Devices." 1993. *Wall Street Journal*, February 10.

Kolata, Gina. 1994. "Scleroderma and Breast Devices: No Tie Is Seen." *New York Times*, May 29.

"Legislative History of the Safe Medical Devices Act of 1990." 1990. *U.S. Code, Congressional and Administrative News*, 101st Cong., 2d Sess., vol. 8, pp. 6305–35.

Littell, Candace L. 1994. "FDA Hang-Ups Stifle Medical Innovations." *Wall Street Journal*, May 17.

Ludwig, Marcia A. 1993. "Physio-Control gets final OK to ship defibrillator." *Journal American* (Bellevue, Wash.), May 20.

"MDMA focuses on FDA process." 1994. *Clinica* 604 (May 23)

"The Medical Device Amendments: 10 Years After." 1986. *FDA Consumer* (May).

"Medical device industry vulnerable to media sensationalism." 1992. *Clinica* 521 (October 7).

"Medical Device Regulation." 1976. *Congressional Quarterly Almanac 1976.*

Merrill, Richard A. 1994. "Regulation of Drugs and Devices: An Evolution." *Health Affairs* 13 (Summer).

Meyers, Mike. 1994. "Losing the edge: Survey shows that state's med-tech pioneers are sending money, jobs, products overseas." *Minneapolis Star Tribune*, June 27.

Mitchell, William C., and Randy T. Simmons. 1994. *Beyond Politics: Markets, Welfare, and the Failure of Bureaucracy.* An Independent Institute book. Boulder, Colo.: Westview Press.

"New Regulations for Medical Devices." 1990. *Congressional Quarterly Almanac 1990*, pp. 579–81.

Newman, Mary. 1994. "To Focus on the Forest: Recognizing the Value of Early Defibrillation Despite Isolated Failures." *Journal of Emergency Medical Services* 19 (May).

"No Improvement in Communication with FDA, Readers Say." 1993. *Devices & Diagnostics Letter*, July 30.

Nobel, Joel J. 1993. Draft of 1993 address to Utah Biomedical Congress.

Olshansky, Jack. 1990. "How the Investment Community Views the Food and Drug Administration's Approval Process and Clinical Outcomes." *Food Drug Cosmetic Law Journal* 45.

Olson, Mary. 1993 (April). "Regulatory Agency Discretion Among Competing Industries: Inside the FDA." Political Economy Working Paper No. 173. Washington University.

Page, Jim. 1992. "Can You Trust Your FDA?" *Journal of Emergency Medical Services* 17 (August).

Pines, Wayne L. 1992. "Handling External Audiences: A Guide for the Medical Device Industry." *Food & Drug Law Journal* 47.

Porter, Elizabeth R. 1994. "David Kessler's High-Wire Act on Enforcement." *Medical Industry Executive* (January).

"Puritan-Bennett Closing Two Manufacturing Facilities Under Consent Decree." 1994. *Medical Devices, Diagnostics & Instrumentation*, January 10.

"Review of 1992." 1993. *Clinica* 533 (January 6).

Schoch, Eric B. 1992. "7 months after shutdown, Lilly awaits FDA ruling to open plant." *Indianapolis Star*, December 6.

Schwartz, John. 1993. "Building New Consensus To Improve Public Safety." *Washington Post*, July 15.

———. 1994a. "FDA Quickly Whittles Down Stack Of Applications for Medical Devices." *Washington Post*, November 29.

————. 1994b. "Mayo study on breast implants raises questions." *Seattle Times* (reprinting *Washington Post*), June 16.

Seigenthaler, John. 1993. "Introduction: Far From the Founding Fathers." In *Bad Prescription for the First Amendment: FDA Censorship of Drug Advertising and Promotion*, ed. Richard T. Kaplar. Washington, D.C.: Media Institute.

Seybert, Adrien. 1994. "Waiting and waiting on the FDA." *Providence Journal*, July 19.

Shapiro, Sidney A., and Joseph P. Tomain. 1993. *Regulatory Law and Policy*. Charlottesville, Va.: Michie Company.

"Siemens Shipment Suspensions Under Consent Decree Affect 8% of U.S. Sales." 1994. *Medical Devices, Diagnostics & Instrumentation*, February 28.

"SOPs Needed as Protection against FDA Criminal Investigations." 1994. *Medical Devices, Diagnostics & Instrumentation*, July 4.

Stout, Hilary, and Rose Gutfeld. 1993. "Vigorous FDA Is Seen as Chief Is Reappointed." *Wall Street Journal*, March 1.

Thottam, Jyoti. 1993. "Generic-Drug Makers Prepare for Their Next Battle: Scandal-Tainted Industry Faces Heightened Competition and Regulation." *Wall Street Journal*, August 9.

U.S. Food and Drug Administration (FDA). 1989 (May). *Regulatory Requirements for Medical Devices*. HHS Pub. FDA 89-4165.

————, Center for Devices and Radiological Health. 1991. "FDA Begins Implementing New Device Legislation." *Medical Devices Bulletin* 9 (May).

———— 1992. "FDA Allowing Limited Use of Silicone Gel-Filled Breast Implants." *Medical Devices Bulletin* 10 (May).

U.S. House of Representatives, Committee on Energy and Commerce, Subcommittee on Oversight and Investigations. 1983 (May). *Medical Device Regulation: The FDA's Neglected Child*. 98th Cong., 1st Sess., Committee Print 98-F.

———— 1993 (May). *Less Than the Sum of Its Parts: Reforms Needed in the Organization, Management, and Resources of the Food and Drug Administration's Center for Devices and Radiological Health*. 103d Cong., 1st Sess., Committee Print 103-N.

"U.S. manufacturers moving out." 1994. *Clinica* 596 (March 28).

"U.S. rethinking device evaluation priorities." 1993. *Clinica* 547/8 (April 21).

"U.S. Surgical Receives FDA Warning Letter For Stapler Product." 1994. *Wall Street Journal*, April 8.

5

Diminishing the Harm

Robert Higgs

E ven if somehow the FDA could be induced to lighten its regulatory burdens and abandon the rules for which costs are especially great in relation to benefits, the longer-term outlook would remain bleak. The underlying problem remains that Congress has given the agency enormously broad and discretionary powers, and the people who control the exertion of those powers—on the surface Kessler and other FDA officials, but more fundamentally the congressional overseers—remain embedded in the same political process. In the words of Richard A. Merrill (1994, 65), former chief counsel at the FDA, "the political climate in which the FDA operates" and "the law under which the FDA functions" fail to "significantly constrain the FDA's appetite for elegant and costly information" and "reward caution and facilitate delay." The next time the news media amplify a shocking revelation with respect to a drug or medical device, all the actors will react in a predictable way. The politicians and the regulators will alter the law and the regulations to demonstrate their deep commitment to protecting the public health, and once again the FDA's powers will be ratcheted upward. So long as the news media and the public continue to play their present roles, the former crying wolf to get an audience and the latter demanding that the federal government serve as an all-purpose protector, the regulated industries will continue to lose what little room for innovative maneuvering they still possess and the well-being of patients will continue to fall short of what it could be in the absence of government regulation.

With the Republican takeover of Congress, the outlook seems somewhat brighter in some eyes. As one reporter observes, "congressional investigations of medical device manufacturers will probably cease" and "attention is likely to turn instead to the regulators" as conservative legislators seek to lighten the industry's regulatory burden ("Future of healthcare" 1994, 7). House Speaker Newt Gingrich's denunciations of the FDA ("bloated" and "Stalinistic") and Commissioner Kessler ("a thug and a bully") have been widely quoted.[1]   One should not expect a revolution, however, merely because Republicans have replaced Democrats as the controlling party in Congress.[2] While the departure of Ted Kennedy, John Dingell, and Henry Waxman from their committee and subcommittee chairmanships promises some relief for the regulated industries and the patients who depend on their products, the Republicans will occupy the same position the Democrats have occupied in the causal structure described in the foregoing chapters. They will face similar incentives and constraints and hence will probably act similarly, especially when faced with some purported "crisis."

If the Republicans were really serious about protecting the public health, they would abolish the FDA, or at least repeal the enabling laws enacted in 1962, 1976, and 1990. So long as those laws remain in force, the FDA—where the same personnel continue to operate—will be extremely difficult to control, and the regulation will be carried out more or less as before. The current legislation, as documented in detail in the foregoing chapters, gives broad discretion to the regulators. FDA officials, with ample assistance from the major news media and other well-placed friends, know how to play the game with Congress to preserve the agency's autonomy and budget.

Of course, any proposal to repeal the drug and device laws enacted in 1962, 1976, and 1990 would elicit cries of astonishment and outrage: How could anyone seriously propose to remove such vital protection of the public health? One can respond to this breathless question in two ways.

First, one can explain and document, as the foregoing chapters do, how the regulatory system *actually* works, as opposed to how the regulators and their friends *claim* it works. Because the protection afforded by the current system is illusory and, indeed, the current system on balance wreaks massive harm, scrapping it would be a blessing to the general public. Absent the FDA, Americans would be healthier and happier.

Whether one can convince the public of this truth is another matter.   Deep-seated prejudices toward believing in beneficent and effective government protection are not easily overcome. Many people have an irrational ideological predisposition to believe that corporations thrive by selling harmful goods to their customers, and that industry and health care providers cannot be trusted with life-and-death matters, whereas government bureaucrats can be.

Such misguided thinking receives constant reinforcement not

only from the efforts of the FDA itself, which conducts a large, continuous public relations effort, but also from the widespread publicity given to the pronouncements of so-called consumer advocacy organizations such as the Health Research Group of Public Citizen. As aptly expressed by C. Frederick Beckner, III;

> Because these consumer groups must persuade the public of the importance of their work in order to stay in business, they need to exaggerate continually their safety concerns as well as the industry's control of the FDA. These groups will consistently argue for very stringent drug control policies. Further, these groups are not in any way accountable to the consumers they claim to represent. Thus, these self-styled public interest groups do not represent the interests of the public as a whole, but instead exploit consumer fear in order to aggrandize the political power necessary for their existence.[3]

Such groups have close contacts with FDA officials and with reporters and editors for major news media. Therefore, they exert considerable influence on public opinion. They can be expected to oppose any reduction of FDA regulatory authority.

Second, with more likelihood of success, one can propose not that the FDA's legislative authority be repealed outright but rather that the laws be modified so that, instead of engaging in excruciatingly detailed rule making and law enforcement, the FDA would be allowed to occupy itself only in product certification. This change would curtail the agency's capacity to do harm while preserving its capacity— on the questionable assumption that it actually has such a capacity—to act beneficially.

After all, as articulated in mainstream (neoclassical) economics, the rationale for FDA-type action rests on an alleged "market failure" having to do with "imperfect information." Specifically, because of the public-good character of information and the asymmetric possession of information by product consumers and producers, consumers are presumed to act on the basis of an "inadequate" amount of information and hence to bear more than the "optimal" amount of risk.[4] If inadequate information is really the problem, then let FDA supply information.

It could issue to products that meet its standards a seal of approval. Consumers would then know that a certified product had passed whatever tests the FDA considered appropriate to demonstrate its safety and efficacy. Consumers would be free, however, to disregard this information if they did not value it. They would be free to purchase products lacking FDA certification, and sellers would be free to sell uncertified products without government obstruction or penalty. Note that *no one would be forced to use products lacking FDA certification.* Sellers could also seek product certification from private testing organizations, whose seals of approval might become more sought after than those of the FDA. Consumers who value FDA testing and other requirements for certification would be able to enjoy any benefits associated with those requirements, while people who have reasons to discount or disregard the ostensible benefits of FDA requirements would not be coerced to act in accordance with the choices made by a handful of bureaucrats in Rockville.

    If government officials really believe they have something of value to the public, then they should be content just to give it to the public. If consumers reject it, their rejection will be a sure sign that they do not value it. There is absolutely no defensible justification for forcing people at gunpoint to do "what's best for them." Such a policy is the most reprehensible form of paternalism. Employing criminal sanctions to treat responsible adult citizens as if they were children is insulting and tyrannical. Citizens who value liberty should have no trouble rejecting a system that simultaneously harms the public health and deprives citizens of their ability to make vital choices about their own health.

Notes

    1. "Bloated" and "Stalinistic" quoted in "Device user fee" 1994, 5; "a thug and a bully" quoted in Schwartz 1995.

    2. Kahan 1995, 19–22, anticipating "continued delayed clearances and the unavailability of many life-saving technologies" (p. 22).

    3. Beckner 1993, 548. The statement applies with equal force to the medical device industry.

    4. On the neoclassical rationale for FDA regulation, see, for example, Stiglitz 1988, 78–79, and Scherer 1993, 98–99, 101. For criticism of the neoclassical rationale, see Higgs 1994a, 3–20.

References

Beckner, C. Frederick, III. 1993. "The FDA's War on Drugs." *Georgetown Law Journal* 82 (December).

"Device user fee bill on hold as GOP gears up for 'aggressive' oversight of FDA premarket program." 1994. *Medical Devices, Diagnostics & Instrumentation,* November 14.

"Future of healthcare reform post-elections." 1994. *Clinica* 630 (November 21).

Higgs, Robert. 1994. "Banning a Risky Product Cannot Improve Any Consumer's Welfare (Properly Understood), with Applications to FDA Testing Requirements." *Review of Austrian Economics* 7.

Kahan, Jonathan. 1995. "US medical device regulation in 1994." *Clinica Review* (January).

Merrill, Richard A. 1994. "Regulation of Drugs and Devices: An Evolution." *Health Affairs* 13 (Summer).

Scherer, F. M. 1993. "Pricing, Profits, and Technological Progress in the Pharmaceutical Industry." *Journal of Economic Perspectives* 7 (Summer).

Schwartz, John. 1995. "Conservative Foes of Government Regulation Focus on the FDA." *Washington Post,* January 21.

Stiglitz, Joseph E. 1988. *Economics of the Public Sector.* 2nd ed. New York: Norton.

About the Authors

RONALD HANSEN is associate dean for academic affairs for the William E. Simon Graduate School of Business Administration at the University of Rochester. He received his Ph.D. in economics from the University of Chicago, and he has taught at Ohio State University, Colgate-Rochester Divinity School, University of Western Ontario, and Lake Forest College. He is member of the board for the Stichting Rochester Graduate School of Management in the Netherlands, economic consultant for the Center for the Study of Drug Development, and a member of the Editorial Board for the *Journal of Research in Pharmaceutical Economics*. He is a contributor to numerous books including *Principles of Pharmaco economics*, *Care and Cost*, *Health Economics*, and *Issues in Pharmaceutical Economics*, and his articles and reviews have appeared in such journals as the *American Journal of Pharmacy*, *Canadian Pharmaceutical Journal*, *Business and Health*, and *Clinical Engineering*.

ROBERT HIGGS is research director for The Independent Institute. He received his Ph.D. in economics from Johns Hopkins University, and he has taught at the University of Washington, Lafayette College, and Seattle University. He has been a visiting scholar at Oxford University and Stanford University, and a fellow for the Hoover Institution and the National Science Foundation. Dr. Higgs is the editor of the Independent Institute book, *Arms, Politics and the Economy*, and the volume, *Emergence of the Modern Political Economy*. His authored books include *The Transformation of the American Economy 1865-1914*, *Competition and Coercion*, and *Crisis and Leviathan*. A contributor to numerous scholarly volumes, he is the

103

author of over 100 articles and reviews in academic journals and many articles in such publications as the *Wall Street Journal* and the *New York Times*.

PAUL H. RUBIN is professor of economics at Emory University and vice president of Glassman-Oliver Economic Consultants. He received his Ph.D. from Purdue University, and he has been professor of economics at Baruch College, chief economist at the U. S. Consumer Product Safety Commission, where he received the 1987 Chairman's Award, head of the Division of Consumer Protection at the Federal Trade Commission, and senior staff economist at the President's Council of Economic Advisors. His authored books include *Tort Reform by Contract*, *Managing Business Transactions*, *Business Firms and the Common Law*, and *Congressmen, Constituents and Contributors*, and he is the editor of *Evolutionary Models in Economics and Law*. His articles and reviews have appeared in such journals as the *Journal of Political Economy*, *Journal of Law and Economics*, *Journal of Legal Studies*, *Journal of Product Liability*, *Journal of Pharmaceutical Economics*, *Public Choice*, *Quarterly Journal of Economics*, and *Yale Journal on Regulation*.

Index